Raising FAITH

D1638028

Helping
our children
find a faith
that lasts

First published in 2018 by Care for the Family in association with Essential Christian.

British Library Cataloguing Data
A catalogue record for this book is available from the British Library.
ISBN: 9780995559615

Designed by Lovely Stuff Studio. *www.lovelystuffstudio.com*
Cover photograph of Adam and Josh Mathias by Innovation Photography.
www.innovation-photography.co.uk
Printed and bound in Great Britain by Xpedient Print Services, Swansea.
www.xpedientprint.co.uk

www.careforthefamily.org.uk

ACKNOWLEDGEMENTS

We have thoroughly enjoyed writing *Raising Faith*, and our hope is that as we ourselves have been inspired and resourced to help our children's faith flourish, the same might be true for you.

Although our names are on the cover, this resource really has been a team effort! We are especially grateful to Sheron Rice for all her brilliant editorial work as she has compiled our writings and helped them flow together. A big thank you to Lisa Higgins for her in-depth research and wisdom, and for managing the process so efficiently. And thank you to Becky Denharder and the Kitchen Table Project team for all their creativity and expertise, and to Katharine's PA, Rachel Harries, for her ongoing support.

A huge thank you to the Lovely Stuff Studio for the great job you have done on design – it's been good working with you. And thank you to Rob Parsons for his foreword and encouragement throughout the writing process.

Finally, special thanks has to go to the Douglas Trust who have invested generously in this vision to help parents inspire faith in their children. Thank you so much!

CONTENTS

Foreword

Not so long ago, I sat down with a church leader who heads up a large number of local churches. We were talking about children coming to faith, and I asked him who he thought was the most important influence in that process. He answered in a heartbeat: 'Parents'.

'That's interesting,' I said. And then I asked him another question: 'How often do your church leaders talk to parents about this in a typical year?' He went white – literally. 'Never,' he said. 'When would they do it? Not on a Sunday morning ...' We lapsed into silence, but our minds were ticking away, and then he looked up at me: 'We've got to do something about this. We've got to work with parents. We've got to talk with them about what they do. We've got to think about this much more.'

The other night, Dianne and I had the joy of having three of our grandchildren stay with us overnight; three little ones aged seven, six, and four. During the evening, we had plenty of fun playing hide-and-seek, watching films, and eating too many sweets (all those things that grandparents can get away with!). The Kitchen Table Project (which we've just launched), has been on my mind so much, and as bedtime was approaching, I switched off the lights, lit a couple of candles, and started to tell them one of the stories of Jesus. They listened, got a bit bored in places, but we got to the end and then said a prayer together. It was nothing spectacular ... but a few more seeds of faith were sown. You see, as a grandparent, I want those kids to find faith. I want them to know the incredible joy of having a relationship with Jesus.

The day suddenly hits us as parents when we realise just how fast our children are growing. In the first 18 years of a child's life, there are

6,570 days. If your child is 10 years old, 3,650 have already gone. It's breathtaking! And God has given us a special role as their parents. He says in the Bible, 'Impress my laws on your children.' Passing on our faith is something that he wants us to do.

If you have little ones, put all you can into them now. You will know the saying, 'Give me a child until he is seven and I will show you the man.' Whether they are toddlers, teenagers or young adults, what we want to do is equip them well for life and let them know that whatever anybody else thinks about them – friends, teachers, employers, social media contacts – they have a Father in heaven who loves them unconditionally.

Raising Faith is incredible because of its simplicity and its determination to help parents of the under-tens plant seeds of faith in their children's lives. Full of practical ideas, it is all about giving children the opportunity to know about God and have a relationship with Jesus.

Saying little prayers together, letting your kids see how you bring your faith into the ordinary things of life – these insignificant things can have a deeper impact that we could ever imagine. My mother could barely read or write, but it was she who taught me to pray. Begin sowing those seeds today. Don't panic and don't lose heart if you've not done much of it so far. It's not too late! And this book is a really good place to get you started.

Rob Parsons, OBE
Founder and Chairman, Care for the Family

Part 1

Where it all begins

I remember it so well: that moment when I left the hospital lobby carrying this tiny baby. I was sure someone was going to stop me.

I was with Jo, my wife, who had just been discharged with our daughter from the maternity ward. I felt like we were imposters. We were totally responsible for the small bundle of life in my arms, yet we felt completely unqualified for the task; we had no idea what to do as parents.

That was five years ago, when our first child was born. We now have another daughter aged three, and I *still* feel underqualified as a dad. As parents, we want our children to grow physically, to be healthy and active. We want them to develop in all kinds of ways, helping them learn how to interact with the world and encouraging them to do their best at school. We want to look after their emotional health, equipping them to deal with feelings such as sadness, frustration, excitement, anger and anticipation. On the relational side, we want to give them the skills to make strong, healthy friendships. And then there is their spiritual life to consider. We want our kids to find faith in a God who loves them, a God who is more committed to them than we can ever be. In discovering a loving relationship with God, our children will find emotional security, purpose in life, and the tools to make good life choices.

As our children grow, we can monitor certain aspects of their development fairly easily – we can see whether they are growing physically and how they are interacting with other children and adults, and their school report will give us an idea of how well they are doing academically. But their spiritual development is much harder to measure.

As parents, are we doing enough to help our children grow in their faith? Are we doing too much? In fact, given the sheer busyness of family life, have we actually been able to give the subject any thought at all?

If our heart's desire as parents is to pass on faith to our offspring, there are a multitude of ways in which we can do this.

How we bring our children up in the faith will be affected by our different circumstances and family background. For example, parents who were both brought up in a Christian home and are now full-time church leaders will have different opportunities to a family where one parent is an ardent atheist and the other is a new Christian without any church background.

And as well as different family situations, we come from different church backgrounds. Our church may be hundreds of years old and hold a very traditional service, or it could be relatively new with informal-style gatherings. It might have a thriving children's ministry or very few kids other than our own. Our church experiences, with their different rituals, rhythms and ways of worshipping, will affect how we put our faith into practice, both personally and in our family life.

Just as there is no one 'correct' way of doing church or being a Christian, there is no one-size-fits-all guaranteed solution to helping our kids develop faith – no such perfect formula exists! Instead, we hope this book will give you some key biblical principles and insights from all church traditions. We will also share a variety of practical ideas you may like to try out with your own family or adapt for them.

Andy

'In discovering a loving relationship with God, our children will find emotional security, purpose in life, and the tools to make good life choices.'

Turning off autopilot

Why do we want our children to find faith?

ANDY

It's very easy to operate on autopilot, going through the motions of life without asking why we do what we do. But when it comes to passing on faith to the next generation, it's important to think through why we might want our children to grow up with a faith in Jesus.

The answer could be very clear to us. For example, we may want our children to have faith in Jesus so that they can be with him in eternity. But there may be a whole range of other reasons as well. We might believe that the Christian faith helps us understand what life is about: our existence is not just a cosmic accident; there is a God who created us and there is a purpose for our lives.

At its core, the Christian faith is packed full of life-affirming values that help us make good choices. As parents, we want our children to be happy, of course, but much more than that, we want them to live life generously, helping others rather than living merely for themselves. Being a follower of Jesus gives us so much. We have a church community to belong to and a sense of our value and worth. We are not defined by our successes and failures but by who we are in Jesus. His death and resurrection has allowed us to be forgiven and adopted into God's family.

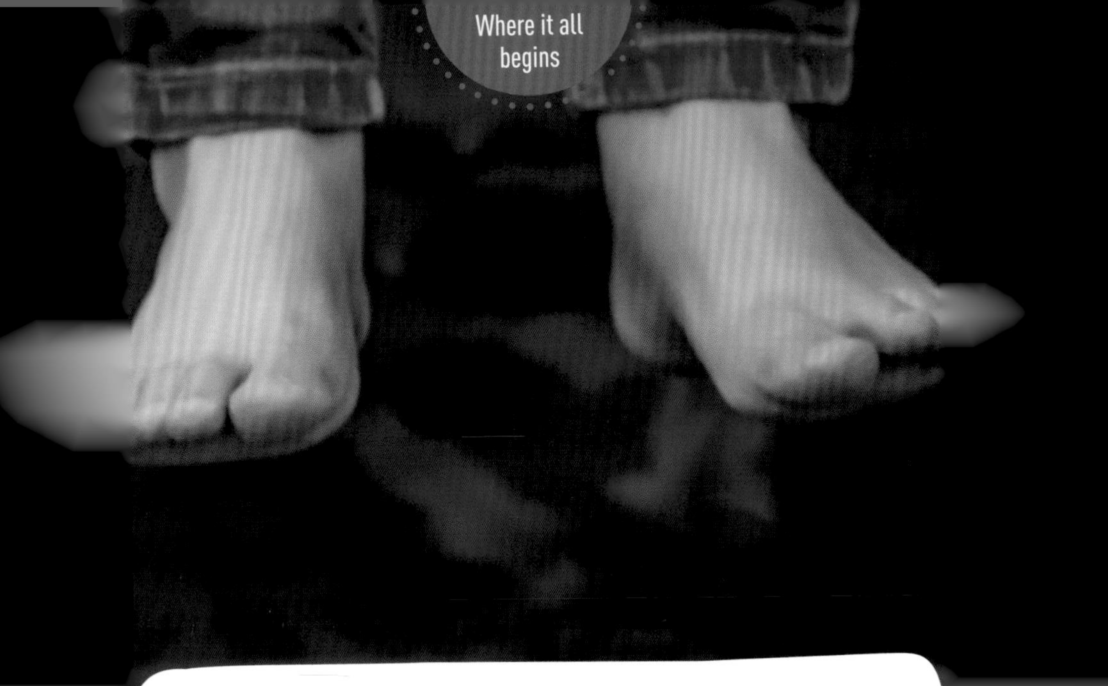

A FATHER IN HEAVEN

One day when my daughter was two years old, she spotted a bouncy castle in the garden of a pub. She wanted to have a go on it (well, what self-respecting two-year-old wouldn't?), so we went in through the gate. As quickly as she could, she took off her shoes and ran up to the castle, her excitement and enthusiasm unmistakable.

As she clambered aboard, from a few metres distance I saw a mean-looking eight-year-old walk up and say something to her. She looked dejected, slid off the castle, and came over to me to explain what had happened: 'He said girls aren't allowed on it.'

Quickly, I told her that she *was* allowed on the bouncy castle, and I walked up alongside her as she climbed back on. With a real confidence about her, she went up to the boy: 'That's my daddy!' she said. And then she started bouncing.

There's something beautiful about that story and the simple words she said because it gives us a snapshot of our Father God. We can't protect our children from all the challenges they'll face in this world – disappointments, ill-health, eight-year-old bullies! – but we *can* help them realise that they have a Father in heaven who is always with them.

That's what I want my children to grow up and discover. I want them to know the God who loves them and will never leave them no matter what trials and tribulations they face.

A divine opportunity

ANDY

Throughout the Bible, there are continual reminders of the importance of passing on the stories of God's faithfulness to the next generation. Psalm 78 talks about teaching our children about why God can be trusted:

'We will tell the next generation the praiseworthy deeds of the Lord, his power, and the wonders he has done ... so that the next generation would know them, even the children yet to be born, and they in turn would tell their children. Then they would put their trust in God and would not forget his deeds but would keep his commands' (Psalm 78:4–7).

And in the New Testament, Paul writes that Timothy, one of the young leaders of the church, had been taught the Scriptures as a child:

'But as for you, continue in what you have learned and have become convinced of, because you know those from whom you learned it, and how from infancy you have known the Holy Scriptures, which are able to make you wise for salvation through faith in Christ Jesus' (2 Timothy 3:14–17).

We might think at first that teaching our children about faith is the job of the Church. After all, when it comes to football, drama or music, we sign our kids up to be coached or taught by an expert, so the danger is that when it comes to passing on the Christian faith, we might simply delegate it to our church, the Sunday school teacher, or the children's worker. In other words, we leave it to the 'professionals'.

Of course, the Church definitely has a role to play, but the Bible suggests that we, as Christian parents, have a God-given duty and opportunity to live out and share our faith with our kids.

ENTERING THE PROMISED LAND

Moses gave a beautiful speech to the Israelites as they prepared to enter the Promised Land. The people were probably feeling both excited and apprehensive: excited as they would soon have a wonderful place in which to settle, but apprehensive because Moses was about to leave them and their relationship with God would change significantly. They would go from being a group of nomads wandering in the wilderness to a people with a homeland. But Moses reminded them of what God had done for them – rescuing them from slavery in Egypt, parting the Red Sea so they could make their escape, and miraculously providing food and water for them in the wilderness.

One of Moses' concerns was that the younger generation had not seen God's work first hand. Because he knew they were about to enter a country whose people did not know God and were involved in evil practices, he insisted that the Israelites passed on the stories of God to their children and grandchildren. In such an environment, it would have been so easy for the new generation to forget all about God.

In Deuteronomy 6:6–9 Moses shared very practically what passing on faith looks like:

'These commandments that I give you today are to be on your hearts. Impress them on your children. Talk about them when you sit at home and when you walk along the road, when you lie down and when you get up. Tie them as symbols on your hands and bind them on your foreheads. Write them on the door-frames of your houses and on your gates' (Deuteronomy 6:6–9).

First, there is the question of 'Who?' – whose role is this? He very clearly did not give this command to the priests (those with religious duties), but to everyone. It's an instruction for us ordinary parents.

Second, there is the issue of 'When?' According to Moses, nurturing our kids' faith is something we can do in everyday life. It shouldn't just happen at church on a Sunday or when our children are at a church children's club. And it's not just for Christmas, Easter or special Christian events. We are asked to pass on our faith when we're sitting with the kids at teatime, walking to play group, getting them ready for bed, dressing them in the morning, or going out on a shopping trip, to Cubs or to Brownies.

MEETING GOD IN EVERYDAY LIFE

Perhaps we have made Sunday morning the only time when we can encounter God and go deeper with him, but when Jesus was with his disciples, he often taught them in the course of their daily activities – when they were fishing, climbing mountains, sharing meals or meeting strangers.

The big question for many of us is 'How?' We know *why* we want to do it, but the *how* is a little more difficult. Moses talked about connecting or 'binding' yourself to God's word, and although we don't need to take this literally as the ancient Hebrews did (they wore a small square leather box containing Scripture verses on their head and arms), we do need to act on the principle underlying it: *we need to get practical.*

Rather than faith being something invisible – something we keep in our hearts – we can show our kids how the God we encounter in the Bible affects our daily lives. We can demonstrate that the heart of the Christian faith is about ordinary people, me and you, living in a relationship with God.

'A God-given responsibility.'

As their parents, we have far more contact time with our children than their Sunday school teacher or youth worker, and for that reason alone we will have far more opportunity to demonstrate how we live out our faith.

The biggest challenge for me is the realisation that as parents, we are being asked to be intentional and purposeful about sharing the reality of Jesus with our kids. It's a God-given responsibility.

KATHARINE

Spiritual growth

Helping our children develop physically, intellectually, emotionally and spiritually

We recently gave our kitchen walls a facelift in Ammonite (aka magnolia – and not a fossil in sight!). We painted all four walls with the exception of a small rectangle just behind the door. This section remains resplendent in its 90s primrose hue and displays a very special height chart that has been etched on the wall in biro and various coloured Sharpie pens over the years. The lowest entry is 'Henry – 3' 10"', who also tops the chart at 6' 3". Perhaps the most entertaining is 'Charlotte' (with a note for the avoidance of doubt) 'with school shoes on'. My father gets a mention twice: 'Pop – 5'10"' and a few years later '5' 8"' (with another note alongside) 'shrunk 2"'! This chart is a treasured family heirloom, and I'm not sure what we'll do if one day we decide to move house.

If the bills every September for new school shoes weren't enough of a cue, our family height chart has been a great reminder that our children *grow*. They grow physically – taller and broader. They grow intellectually, first beginning to recognise colours, then numbers and letters, until they are able to read entire stories for themselves. And they grow emotionally too. Parents of toddlers take heart: the temper tantrum in the supermarket or the meltdown over the fact that there are 'bits' in the bread really won't last forever.

As parents, we take the responsibility for our children's physical development in our stride. We visit the clinic for our babies to be weighed and have their growth plotted on the centile chart; we disguise broccoli in an attempt to get them to eat their five a day; and we take them on a bike ride or to the park to give them exercise. We help them to learn by reading to them, testing them on spellings and helping with sums. We also try to influence their emotional development, suggesting that rather than hitting their sister, they kick a football hard at the wall, and we try to help them manage a perceived unfairness. But although we are generally on the front foot in encouraging our children's physical, intellectual and emotional growth, we can sometimes overlook the fact that we also have an important role to play in encouraging them to grow spiritually.

A HOST OF INFLUENCES

Of course, as we've mentioned earlier, this is something we may not have considered at all, or we may have other concerns. I was having coffee with a mum who had been along to the toddler group at church and was curious about the Christian faith. While there were many things that attracted her, one of her worries was the thought that if she began introducing her children to church she might be brainwashing them. She said she wanted them to be 'free to choose for themselves' without any pressure from her. As we chatted, I said that, like it or not, from their earliest days our children's thinking is being shaped. Their family background, friendships, TV/internet viewing habits – all their experiences of life – will have an impact on their thinking. A host of influences – people, organisations, marketing companies – target our children's minds. We are not on an even playing field, and to be fair to our children we need to overcome any inertia we might have and make sure that we give them information about the Christian faith and the opportunity to make a choice for themselves. Sharing our faith with them is not just a matter of, as one parent said, 'being sure my child gets into heaven', but of putting deep values into their lives that will counter the message that they can only be loved if they achieve certain things or look a certain way. If ever a generation needed to grasp the unconditional love of God, it is this one. In his gospel, Luke makes an interesting observation about Jesus as a young boy:

'Jesus grew in wisdom and stature, and in favour with God and man' (Luke 2:52).

I have no doubt that his parents were praying for that, and we can be praying the same too for our children. Encouraging their spiritual growth, as well as their growth in all the other ways, is a task worthy of our very best effort.

'If ever a generation needed to grasp the unconditional love of God, it is this one.'

Getty Images

KATHARINE

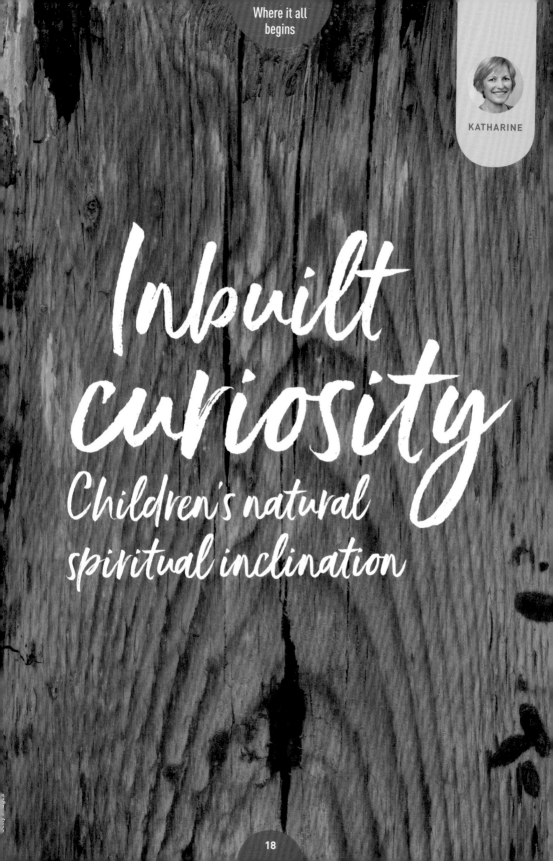

Inbuilt curiosity

Children's natural spiritual inclination

We had the beach all to ourselves and walked up and down it, surveying the damage caused by the previous night's storm. The shoreline was littered with seaweed, jellyfish, plastic bottles, fishing nets, and a solitary green flip-flop; the wind had taken no prisoners. Our mission for the morning was to uncover among the debris a large piece of driftwood that we could use to make a mantelpiece. I had seen examples on Pinterest that made it look easy and was sure that my husband Richard could rise to the challenge! We returned triumphant some time later carrying the perfect specimen. *Woodworking for Dummies* and a nifty YouTube tutorial to hand, he set to work. The main advice seemed to be to plane in line with the grain of the wood as this gives a smooth clean surface. Cutting against the grain will make the wood splinter and cause endless grief.

In his book *Born Believers*, psychologist and anthropologist Justin Barrett uses this as an analogy to describe children's natural inclination to believe in God. He argues that as parents we are 'working with the grain of the universe' when we talk to our children about faith. They are predisposed to believe in a supernatural God who can bring order and meaning to their lives.

Our children are older now, but when they were little, a favourite game involved playing at being superheroes. One of our boys practically lived in a Superman outfit for over a year (saving a lot on the family clothes bill!). His friend lived in a Batman outfit and together they had many superpowers that equipped them to save the world. Emma, a mum of three said:

'Like most children, my daughters have wonderful imaginations. One has an imaginary friend called Minky who is rarely far from her side. Minky walks to school with her, goes on play dates with her, and sits next to her in the car. And my daughter often asks us to lay a place for her at the meal table.'

'Being able to see beyond the purely physical seems to come naturally to children.'

Being able to see beyond the purely physical seems to come naturally to children.

I am slightly embarrassed to admit to my powers of invention as a child: I would play a game with my brother when I would be God. This allowed me to be 'in charge' for the duration of the game and demand that he (and my other two siblings on occasions) act at my bidding. While there was nothing wrong with my imagination, both my theology and inflated ego obviously needed addressing!

The apostle Paul wrote to the church in Rome that God is clearly seen in nature:

'For since the creation of the world God's invisible qualities – his eternal power and divine nature – have been clearly seen, being understood from what has been made' (Romans 1:20).

Throughout the ages, even the most primitive cultures have had a belief in an all-powerful god or gods who rule their lives, and it is only in 21st century Western culture that this belief is no longer normal. From a young age, children have much to make sense of in creation. Why are trees always green and the sky blue? Who decides when the sun goes to bed and the moon and the stars get up? Why is water wet? What is infinity? Who made you, and who made me? (And that's just for starters!) As parents, in attempting to answer these big questions about life, we can highlight the wonder of creation, and we can signpost our children to a supernatural creator who is all-powerful, all-knowing, and all-good – the God who brings meaning and order to their lives.

We are also working with the natural order of creation in conveying to our little ones the concept of grace. There was always much excitement and anticipation when our four children were little and Granny was coming to stay. I'd like to say it was because they were so looking forward to spending time with her, but nearer the truth was the fact that she would arrive laden with a monstrous bag of pick and mix sweets for each of them. Oblivious to any warnings about tooth decay, little fingers would tear open the bags with delight and excitement. It would be impossible to imagine them (or any other child for that matter) protesting and telling their grandmother, 'You really shouldn't have ...' or giving the sweets back because 'I really don't deserve them.' Unlike many adults, children don't feel the pressure to reciprocate or earn gifts, they simply welcome them with open arms. In the same way, they have little problem in embracing the concept of the wonderful undeserved gift of grace.

As parents, we are working with the grain of the universe in inspiring faith in our children. We have everything to play for!

'As parents, we are working with the grain of the universe in inspiring faith in our children.'

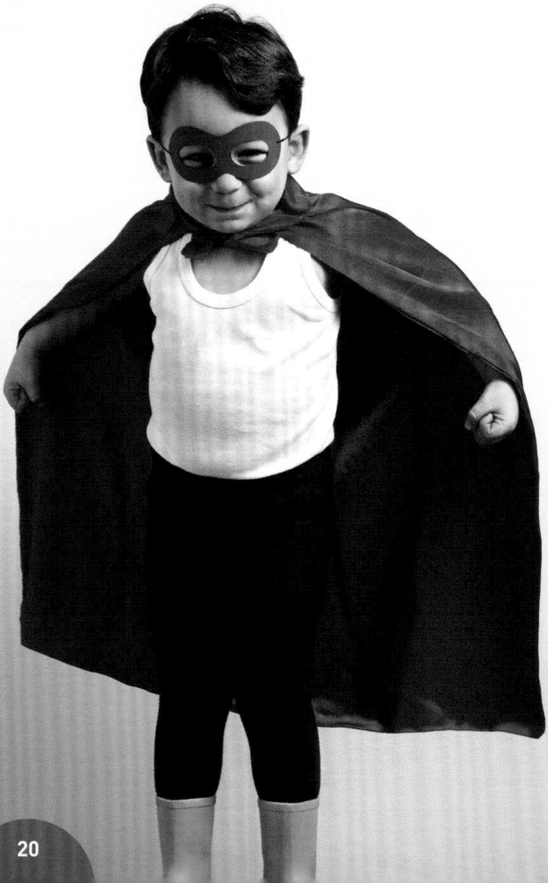

Getty Images

KATHARINE

Stages of faith

Four building blocks in spiritual development

Innovation Photography

Every parent will have hopes and dreams for their child. We may see them as future astronauts, brain surgeons, master bakers, Premier League footballers, or winners of the Nobel Peace prize, or perhaps we have more modest aspirations for their lives. But as Christian parents, many of us will have another, overriding, hope and dream for our children: the longing that they grow up to have a living faith of their own.

In the book of Proverbs, there is a lovely reassuring verse: 'Start children off on the way they should go, and even when they are old they will not turn from it' (Proverbs 22:6). We'd love to believe this is a promise of how things will end up if we do all the right things as parents. But Proverbs, like other wisdom literature in the Bible, tells us how things *generally* turn out – so this verse is a principle, not a guarantee. As parents, we can't take total responsibility for our children's spiritual life; that is too heavy a burden for us to bear.

Having said that, there are so many important things we *can* do to encourage faith and make it easier for our children to love God.

THE BUILDING BLOCKS OF FAITH

A model suggested by John Westerhoff III in his book *Will Our Children Have Faith?* is that in general there are four distinct stages in our children's spiritual development.

1 EXPERIENCED FAITH

This stage is about our children's first exposure to Christianity. For children of Christian parents they will experience how we choose to live out our faith at home and see this as 'normal'. They might have Bible stories read to them, prayers said with them, and be taken to church.

How our children experience faith in their early years will shape how they see God in later life. My father is a loving, generous man and that has influenced my understanding of God. Those whose fathers (or father-figures) are angry or demanding will have a different experience at home that will also influence their view of what God is like.

This stage of experienced faith is a vital one. When we've asked our toddler to put on their shoes for the hundredth time with nil response we might be forgiven for thinking they don't listen to us. But quite the reverse is true: our children don't miss a thing! So giving them a positive experience of faith includes making it part of our everyday lives and everyday conversations. At this stage, it is often said that 'Faith is more easily caught than taught.' Our priorities, our reactions when we are disappointed or let down, how we spend our money, how we treat others, our attitude to church will all form their experience of faith.

2 AFFILIATIVE FAITH

This stage is similar to experienced faith in that it involves our child joining in with what others do around them. Peer groups at this stage are vital. While we may want our children to have a diverse range of friends from different backgrounds and beliefs, it's important as well to encourage friendships with those who share our faith. We can invite children from other Christian families to tea, get involved in a church with good children's work and leaders who really care for them, or go as a family to one of the Christian festivals.

When children are having a good time with people who love God we make it easier for them to feel they belong, and this can be a significant factor in them finding a faith of their own. For the last 15 years, we have been away for half-term with two other families: six adults, twelve children and three dogs making up the party. It has been a logistical feat to arrange, but looking back it has provided our children with an opportunity to experience and join in with faith lived out in the lives of friends. The focus has been on family and fun. We've jumped off high rocks into the sea, watched box sets on TV while it's been raining, been swimming and surfing in the freezing water off the Cornish coast, gone on walks with children protesting that their legs were tired, played beach cricket and taken over many pubs and cream-tea shops along the way. Those times together allowed some of the children to form lifelong friendships that I believe have played a major part in shaping their journey of faith.

'As parents, we can't take total responsibility for our children's spiritual life; that is too heavy a burden for us to bear.'

3 SEARCHING FAITH

The third building block of faith is the searching stage. This is when children begin to ask questions, make sense of and understand the faith they've been taught. It can be a daunting phase for us as parents: how do we begin to answer the tough questions that we may not even have answers for ourselves? Questions such as: 'Where was God at the bombing in the Ariana Grande concert in Manchester?', 'Why hasn't God healed my best friend of cancer?', 'Why hasn't God helped the refugee children who have nowhere to live?'

As parents, we want our children's relationship with God to be easy and straightforward, but the truth is that their journey of faith will inevitably involve some doubts and disappointments along the way. We don't have to provide neat, watertight answers to their questions, and it's fine to let them know that some questions won't be answered this side of heaven. Inviting their thoughts, encouraging discussion and debate, and giving them plenty of space for questions, doubts and wonderings will help them on to the final stage in the faith journey.

'We don't have to provide neat, watertight answers to their questions, and it's fine to let them know that some questions won't be answered this side of heaven.'

4 OWNED FAITH

This is when a child comes to a real and personal faith of their own. They may still have doubts and questions, and they may face difficulties ahead in living out their faith, but they have a living relationship with God that is a reality in their lives. Some children come to that place at the age of twelve or even younger. But, ultimately, faith they don't own themselves won't survive.

Recognising the building blocks of faith and understanding which stage our children are at will help us find new ways to encourage, inspire and cheer them on to discover a relationship with God for themselves.

Just one last thought about stages of faith: you may be a parent of older children and your heart is breaking because, despite your best endeavours, your children have not yet come to that place of owned faith. They may still be searching for answers or have decided (for the time being) to choose a different path. The aim of this book is, of course, to encourage us as parents to realise the difference we can make in our children's early years to their finding faith for themselves, however, as we have already said, there are no guarantees. But whatever our situation and whatever stage our children are at on the journey of faith, we can continue to play our part in nurturing it. We can pray and hold on to the knowledge that God, their heavenly Father, loves them passionately and longs for them to put their trust in him.

Personality and spirituality

Discovering how our kids best connect with God

KATHARINE

It's Tuesday afternoon in primary school and time for Year 2's art lesson. The teacher walks around the classroom admiring the children's work. 'What are you painting?' she asks one little girl who is concentrating hard on her picture.

'I'm drawing God.'

The teacher pauses and then says, 'But no one knows what God looks like.'

Without looking up from her painting, the girl replies, 'Well, they will in a minute!'

In her own mind, that little girl knew exactly what God was like, but faith is not one-size-fits-all! Each of our children will have a different way of seeing God and relating to him.

In his book *Sacred Pathways*, author Gary Thomas describes the wonderful variety of ways in which we relate to God according to our different personalities. We may enjoy lively worship or prefer quiet contemplation; we may love a good Bible study and thrive on intellectual thought; we may express our faith by serving and helping others; we may encounter God best through creation – a walk in the great outdoors feeding our soul.

'Each of our children will have a different way of seeing God and relating to him.'

But it's not just grown ups who relate to God in different ways; children, too, will have their own way of expressing their love for him. As parents, we know our children's personalities; we have time to study them, and we can encourage them to express their love for God according to the unique way he has made them. It might be through music – fun CDs with little ones performing energetic actions in the kitchen or older children strumming a guitar along to a worship album. They may connect with God when they are on their own in their room, out on a bike ride, or a family walk. Or perhaps they feel close to him when they are with friends or when they are drawing or doing craft.

WHAT MAKES THEM TICK

A word of warning! Don't confuse your child's personality with their spirituality. As a mum of three high-spirited boys (and one high-spirited girl) who didn't like sitting still at church or doing things with glitter and glue in Sunday school, when I realised this truth, I found it so freeing. We may have inherited set ideas on what activities best help children learn about God, and so we assume they aren't interested in spiritual things if they don't want to do them. But they may not like an activity because it simply doesn't fit their personality. So let's take a step back and look at what makes our children tick, what fires their imagination, and what they enjoy doing. Once we've done that, we can then encourage the things that will best help them connect with God in their heart.

The Olympic athlete and missionary Eric Liddell, whose story inspired the film *Chariots of Fire*, famously said, 'I believe God made me for a purpose, but he also made me fast. And when I run, I feel his pleasure.' Let's watch for the things that enable our children to feel God's pleasure in their hearts, and let's encourage them in it.

Getty Images

Part 2

Family matters

'The place where the unconditional love of our Father in heaven can be modelled for us.'

At our Care for the Family parenting events, we always begin by acknowledging that families come in all shapes and sizes. There will be those who are parenting as couples, those who are co-parenting, single parents, foster carers, adoptive parents, grandparents, kinship carers, step-parents, and more still. Each family has its own set of challenges, but whatever the situation, every parent or carer will want to do their utmost to bring up their children in a safe, stable, and nurturing environment.

Strong families are at the heart of strong communities, and strong communities are at the heart of a strong society. God has designed it this way. God's nature is relational; he loves it when we spend time with him, and he made us to enjoy relating with others too. Throughout the Bible, God worked through families who more often than not got things wrong, but were used by him to bring about his purposes anyway. Jesus was, of course, born into a family and experienced the joys and challenges of everyday family life.

A PLACE OF PROTECTION

The family is designed to be a place of nurture where we learn key lessons for living. It's where we can discover how to relate to each other, understand different points of view, and experience different personalities. And it's where we can learn to forgive and be forgiven, to love and to be loved. The family should be a place of protection – a harbour against the storms of life. It is where we often experience our greatest sorrows but also our biggest triumphs. And, importantly, it is the place where the unconditional love of our Father in heaven can be modelled for us.

Katharine

A firm foundation

The importance of trust, warmth, love and security in the home

KATHARINE

Research has shown that one of the key elements in passing on faith to children is the warmth of the relationships in the home. And building a warm relationship with our children begins from the day that they are born. In the 1960s, psychologist John Bowlby developed what is now considered one of the most important theories of child development: attachment theory. This says that the quality of the relationship between a child and their primary caregiver (generally the parent) is vital for the child's healthy development.

As a parent responds to a baby's needs (picking them up and cuddling them when they cry, feeding them, smiling back at them when they smile, and being there for them to return to after they've explored the world), bonds of emotional and physical attachment are formed that give the child a blueprint of how relationships in life work. Advances in technology have enabled us to discover that the quality of this nurturing relationship actually affects a child's brain development. Sobering pictures demonstrate the shockingly smaller and less developed brains of children who have suffered severe neglect compared to those of children who have been nurtured and loved. A positive attachment will affect our children throughout their lives, giving them a secure base from which they can learn to trust others, seek new experiences, and ultimately know that they are loved and lovable.

Building strong bonds of attachment and warmth is not only good news for our children's emotional development; it also helps us as we seek to build a foundation of faith in their lives.

As parents, we have the opportunity to model the unconditional love that God, the perfect parent, has for each of his children. By creating an environment in the home where they experience trust, warmth, love and security in their lives, we will make it a small step for them to recognise these very things in the heart of God.

'Research has shown that one of the key elements in passing on faith to children is the warmth of the relationships in the home.'

Innovation Photography

KATHARINE

What's your parenting style?

Three different approaches – and the best one to aim for

At our Care for the Family events for parents, one of the sessions that people find most helpful is when we talk about different styles of parenting. Understanding the different styles and adopting the right one helps us navigate the ups and downs of family life but is also key in respect of how we encourage our children on a journey of faith.

Experts agree that there are basically three styles of parenting. The way we ourselves were brought up and our temperament and personality will often influence which style comes most naturally to us.

Getty Images

1 AUTHORITARIAN

At one end of the spectrum is the authoritarian style. Authoritarian parents are often perfectionists and like to be in control. They have high expectations of their children and there are lots of rules in the home that are all enforced rigidly with strict consequences for anyone stepping over the line. There is little or no room for negotiation. A typical Sunday morning in the authoritarian home involves breakfast promptly at 8.00 am, the children wearing clothes that were picked out or approved by the parent the night before. Hair needs to be brushed, shoes cleaned and shirts tucked in. Sunday morning worship is compulsory. Any requests from a child to miss church so that they can go to a friend's special birthday treat are flatly refused with no room for manoeuvre.

This sheep and pen picture illustrates the authoritarian style of parenting. It is true that this style brings clarity – everyone knows what is and isn't allowed, and there's no danger of any ambiguity or misunderstanding. However, the disadvantage is that children can feel hemmed in, suffocated and even resentful because there is no room for independent thought, creativity and discovery.

2 PERMISSIVE

Right at the other end of the spectrum lies the permissive style. Children of permissive parents may be the envy of their peers – their parents' style is hands-off and laid-back. There are few rules and few consequences even if these are crossed.

Breakfast in this family's home on Sunday morning is as and when people want it – if a child is running late it could be a chocolate biscuit as they head out of the front door. There is freedom to choose what to wear whatever their age and whatever the occasion. Church is just one among a variety of activities on offer that morning alongside watching TV, ten-pin bowling or playing with a friend – the children are free to choose.

The sheep standing in the open hills illustrates this permissive style of parenting. Children are free – they have plenty of opportunity to be creative and forge independence, but what they don't have is security. Guidance and boundaries are important for our children not just for discipline but so that they feel safe.

3 ASSERTIVE

The third style of parenting is assertive and is the one preferred by the experts. It is illustrated by this picture where the sheep has room to explore but can clearly see where the boundary is. The gate is open to allow it to explore and discover things, but there is always a safe pen for it to come back in when it needs to.

Assertive parents know that setting boundaries is important for a child's safety and sense of security, but they will set as few rules as possible. They are 'firm but fair', choosing their battles carefully, saying no to the things that really matter and yes to everything else. The boundaries are set in the context of a warm parent-child relationship, and there is room for negotiation and manoeuvre on both sides. So in this home on Sunday morning, breakfast and going to church together as a family is planned and expected, but lost socks, late nights and general family mayhem are taken into account. If children want to wear a football strip or princess outfit to church then so be it. And a request to miss church for a best friend's party is discussed together and negotiated.

Innovation Photography

A WARM, LOVING RELATIONSHIP

While the assertive parenting style is the one to aim for, as parents we need to be kind to ourselves. We will all be able to think of occasions when we have either been too draconian, laying down the law too strictly, or when we've taken our eye off the ball and been too relaxed about a particular issue. Alongside the rules we give our children is the need to build a warm, loving relationship with them; it's been wisely said that 'rules without relationship lead to rebellion'. Through that loving relationship, we will be modelling to them the way God, our heavenly Father, parents us.

Adopting the right parenting style sounds neat and easy on paper, but it's worth remembering that life *isn't* neat. In particular, those with challenging parenting issues, including those who are raising children with additional needs, may find they need to do things a little differently. Nevertheless, the general principles hold good whatever our situation.

Five ways of showing love

ANDY

We all want our children to know that they are loved unconditionally – to realise that we love them no matter what (even if, at certain points in time, that's hard to put into practice!). This means that our love doesn't come with strings attached – strings such as: if they do well at school/if they get selected to play in the sports team/if they get the haircut we want them to have ... When children grow up in a loving home, they thrive. Research shows that children who know they are loved learn more effectively, are more positive, and are much easier to discipline.

LOVE LANGUAGES

The challenge we have is that the ways in which we, as parents and carers, show our love for our children might be different to how *they* understand love. And what communicates love to one child may not be received in the same way by another child. Authors Gary Chapman and Ross Campbell in their book *5 Love Languages for Children* have put forward the idea that there are five distinct ways in which people give and receive love. They call these 'love languages'. Once children reach around five, six or seven years of age, they will probably begin to best communicate love in one or more of these particular languages. Here's a brief description of each one.

1

WORDS OF AFFIRMATION

Compliments and encouraging words go a long way with children – they thrive on praise! Our words can focus on personality, accomplishments or anything else that affirms them. This is not just about praising a child's achievement and behaviour, but appreciating them for the unique and special person they are.

TIPS

- Leave a note under their pillow saying you love them.
- Write encouraging messages on the mirror.
- Give them compliments.
- Praise them in front of other people.
- Write a letter to them.
- Put a supportive note in their lunchbox on a challenging day.

2

QUALITY TIME

Quality time is about undivided attention. Your child may understand love in this way if they like having your undivided attention or having you watch them while they are playing. When they are babies, we play on the floor with them; as they get older, we can give them quality time by having conversations, playing in the park, or reading bedtime stories. If there are siblings in the house or we have a very busy work schedule, it's important to create some one-to-one alone time with them.

For single parent mums and dads this can all be much harder. Don't go on a guilt trip, but just grab those moments whenever possible.

TIPS

- Go out for a milkshake or go on a special trip together.
- Read together.
- Sit next to each other when watching a film.
- Ask about their day, making eye contact.

3

GIFTS

Children with this love language adore having gifts; for them they are a visible sign of love. It's not about the cost and the size of the present, and they don't have to be given every day, but recognising that this is a key way of making this particular child feel loved is an important factor in communicating our love.

TIPS

- Keep a small stash of inexpensive gifts to give them now and again – not just on birthdays or at Christmas.
- Show that you are thinking about them when you are away by bringing back a small present for them.
- Give them things like shells from the beach or an interesting stone.

4

ACTS OF SERVICE

This is your child's love language if they like people doing nice things for them. Of course, parents are constantly doing practical things to help their children – and we want to be kind and helpful to them all the time – but this is about knowing which acts are *particularly* important to them, rather than saying yes all the time. For example, have we noticed that they really appreciate it when we help them with homework or teach them to perform a certain task?

TIPS

- Help them to choose a new outfit.
- Offer to drive them somewhere in the car when they usually get the bus.
- Clean their bike for them.
- Help them study for a test.

5

TOUCH

There's an incredible emotional power in physical touch. We know that babies need to be held and cuddled and, as children grow up, many still understand love through physical affection. Most children of course, especially younger ones, like to be hugged (and we shouldn't stop doing that if we notice that our child particularly appreciates receiving words of affirmation), but to a child with this love language, things like a simple touch on the arm, a pat on the back and a hug are especially important.

TIPS

- Sit your child on your lap for story time.
- Snuggle down under a duvet to watch a movie.
- Have a tickle fight.
- Hold hands and hug often.

Children need to know they are loved on their terms, but it can be tricky trying to determine your child's preferred love language. Try observing how they themselves show love to others and listen to their requests and complaints. As they get older, it becomes easier to spot their love language if you look out for it.

I found that my eldest would often complain about not getting to do things alone with Jo or me. It slowly dawned on us that she might best receive love in having quality time – time when she got our undivided attention. We have since made it a weekly routine for me to take her for a run in the park so that we can jog and chat together. And my youngest loves physical contact. Jo and I have watched how she will take any opportunity to climb on us and wrap herself up in our arms. Again, since noticing this, we have tried to see how we can incorporate more physical touch when we interact with her. When we say goodbye after dropping her off at nursery, we are particularly intentional about giving her a warm hug as we tell her we love her before we leave.

'Try observing how they themselves show love to others and listen to their requests and complaints.'

You know your own child better than anyone, so you are in the best place to assess their main love language. Particularly if your child has additional needs, there may also be some things that you will *avoid* doing as you know they will find it difficult.

While it's good to focus on our child's main love language, it's important to remember to use the other four as well. Although our children receive love best from one or two languages, they will always benefit from *all* the ways in which we show them unconditional love.

Innovation Photography

'We Always ...'

Family traditions

KATHARINE

I was at a summer conference and the appearance of the sun after several days of torrential rain had brought people out in their shorts and shades. The lure of ice creams resulted in a queue which seemed to rival those for rides at Alton Towers. We took our place behind a young dad and his girls and began chatting. Before long, the conversation had turned into a debate about the pros and cons of salted caramel versus wildberry shortcake, waffle cone versus plain, and sprinkles versus flakes. One of the girls told us that her favourite was 'unicorn' ice cream – multi-coloured, multi-flavoured, and made every Friday night by their mum. 'We *always* have it,' she said.

If you ask someone to describe happy memories of their childhood, it won't be long before those two words come up: we always. 'We always ... had doughnuts after school on Fridays/climbed a hill on New Year's Day/had an Easter egg hunt in the garden.' Looking back to our own childhood, maybe most of us can add our own *we always* ... to the list.

Family traditions are important. They give a sense of connectedness and identity and make us feel we *belong*. Identity matters. We are the Hills, and as Team Hill we will do things in particular ways and have particular values that are important to us. Our family traditions are a key part of that.

FAMILY CELEBRATIONS

Some traditions just happen and others we create more deliberately – birthdays, Christmas and other celebrations are a great opportunity to create some of these. Last Christmas I decided to clear out our box of decorations, many going back to items the children made when they were little. A lot of these were looking tired, and a foray on Pinterest had led me to believe a more sophisticated look was required. I bought some new colour-themed baubles and white lights, banned tinsel, and set to work. My efforts – which rivalled those of *Ideal Home* magazine – were not appreciated by team Hill. There was uproar! Apparently we *always* have a tree with Ed's robin (only half a beak), Charlotte's angel (a damaged wing), Henry's reindeer (easily mistaken for a donkey), and George's Father Christmas (definitely seen better days). It seems that Christmas isn't a 'Hill Christmas' without them. Our children won the day and the bedraggled cosmopolitan array of decorations remains safely tucked away ready for next year.

Other traditions around Christmas include putting up a lovely advent calendar that we bought when the children were little. It takes pride of place on a chest in our hall and contains 24 little books, each one telling a small part of the Christmas story. Granny would always come up trumps with a chocolate advent calendar, and while each day's contents were devoured before breakfast (against all rules), we would also try to read that day's part of the story together. Sometimes peace and harmony reigned and it worked beautifully. At other times, there would be a crisis over a lost reading book, a rugby scrum on the floor, or one child at least refusing to cooperate. Our four children are all grown now, but that advent calendar is still

> ***'Family traditions are important. They give a sense of connectedness and identity and make us feel we belong.'***

an important part of sharing the Christmas story together, and I wouldn't be surprised if they do a similar thing if they have children of their own.

Many families have birthday traditions such as a special song, cake, crown, or chair. In Proverbs it says that words have the power of life (Proverbs 18:21). Birthdays are a great opportunity to write some encouraging words to our child. We can point out something we love about them, something they have done well, something in their character that we know reflects the heart of God. We can remind them how he sees them and encourage them to discover the great plans he has for their lives. I recently sent an encouraging card to someone who was not used to receiving words like this and she was moved to tears. My daughter saw her reaction and commented, 'Has Mum written something in your card? She *always* does that!' It seems even this has become a tradition.

'Words have the power of life.'

SECURITY AND A SENSE OF BELONGING

Meal times can be a great opportunity for developing traditions, and eating together on a regular basis is important. Overlapping schedules, high chairs and pureed carrots, big chairs and roast beef, and a range of bedtimes can make it difficult, but if we find some time to sit down together, even just a couple of times a week, it's a wonderful way to connect, build identity, and reinforce a sense of belonging. Richard and I would try to say grace with the children at mealtimes to thank God for the food, and a big, fun wooden dice helped reluctant pray-ers to join in. There was a short grace on each side of the dice, and it was always a popular task to be the one to roll it.

We've had many family traditions over the years, some that lasted just for a short while and some that have endured. But each one has created for our children that sense of family identity, security, love and belonging that reflects the heart of God, and they have provided good soil for the seeds of faith to be planted and to grow.

ANDY

This thing called faith

We can take encouragement from the fact that inspiring faith in our children is not only about teaching them or giving them information about what we believe. In his book *Children Finding Faith*, Francis Bridger helpfully describes the concept of faith by breaking it down into four verbs: believing, trusting, doing and imagining.

1 FAITH AS BELIEVING

'Believing' faith is about knowledge and facts – what we believe intellectually about the doctrines that underpin our faith. The Anglican church service recognises the importance of this when the congregation says the Creed together: 'I believe ...'

2 FAITH AS IMAGINING

'Imagining' faith is about seeing the way of life that God has called us to. The imagination has often been undervalued because it is both personal and subjective. We have an imagination because we are made in the image of the creative God, and our imagination enables us to picture what it looks like to live out our faith.

3 FAITH AS TRUSTING

'Trusting' faith is about accepting the character of God, believing that he is faithful. Ultimately, it is not words and statements, doctrines and creeds that we believe in, but a person: the person of God. So we don't want to encourage our children to blindly follow rules, but to discover that God can be trusted. Faith like this grows through our experiences and encounters with God.

4 FAITH AS DOING

'Doing' faith is about putting our beliefs into action: 'Faith by itself, if it is not accompanied by action, is dead' (James 1:17). It is not a dormant kind of thing – something that we leave in the background of our lives. It is an action word. A verb. It is a *do-able* thing that expresses our love for God. When we put our faith into action, we bring it alive.

When these four aspects of faith are combined we can see that a life of faith will demonstrate what we believe, what we imagine, who we put our trust in, and what we do.

The beautiful thing is that the family unit allows us to explore these aspects of faith with our children. As adults, especially if we have been Christians for some time, we will probably have more knowledge about Christian doctrines and the Bible – who wrote the different books, why, when and to whom – so we can help teach our children to build a believing faith of their own. If we are new Christians, we can go on a journey of exploration together with our children.

When it comes to imagining faith, children are often much better at this than we are, conjuring up the dramas of Bible stories, the characters, atmosphere, tastes and smells. As adults, we can often box God up according to our experiences, but children have an innate ability to imagine God doing what we think is impossible. In their paintings of God, they often reveal insights that we have missed; they have a faith that is not limited by what they can see in front of them. As they imagine what God sees and feels in a certain scenario, they can help us connect with his heart. The wonderful thing about children's imagination is that when we play with them, encouraging them to imagine things, we are actually helping build the ability to have faith.

'They learn that they can trust their mum and dad, and that helps them feel that they can trust God too.'

The very nature of family life means that our children experience a trust relationship from an early age. As their parents, we lovingly look after them, giving them food, warmth, affection, and comfort. This powerfully communicates what it is to trust. They learn that they can trust their mum and dad, and that helps them feel that they can trust God too.

And the learning process is two-way. I find that as I pray to God, I can put in a lot of caveats: 'Please God, would you do this ... if you can ... if it's not too much bother ...' Yet, I am learning afresh from my kids the expectancy that God hears their prayers and will answer them.

Finally, we can model faith as doing in both the values and the practices we adopt in our home. For example, when we strive to put things right after an argument, we are giving our children lessons in forgiveness and reconciliation. And when we pray as a family, we are demonstrating not just the doing aspect of faith, but the fact that we are trusting God with all things. We can share with our children practical aspects of our faith such as giving to people in need and visiting those who are lonely. In doing faith as a family, we are journeying together, learning from and inspiring each other in our walk with God.

Part 3

Access all areas

I grew up in a Christian home with both my parents working as church leaders. I remember one summer that my dad wanted to write a devotional book for families that would be a model of how best to do family quiet times. Of course, it was us, his own family, who he planned to use as guinea pigs for his ideas: we would do quiet times together, and then he could share with the world the wisdom he'd gained from that practical experience.

But it was the summer holidays, and sitting down and studying the Bible together with our parents wasn't top of my brother's and my priority list! In fact, it was the last thing we wanted to do. School was out, and we wanted to be out on the beach playing, running around the garden, chasing a football, or chilling out and watching TV. There were a few awkward moments as my dad tried to convene the family around the kitchen table, but time and time again his best efforts failed. The family devotional book never did get written!

We often have this warped idea of the perfect Christian family. We might imagine them all getting up at 5.00 am for an hour of prayer then meeting for a Bible study on Leviticus before breakfast. And, of course, there are never any arguments or wasted hours spent in front of the TV. As a family, they make every effort to compromise and submit to each other, and they spend their spare time raising money for Tearfund and door-knocking their street with evangelistic leaflets.

OK, I exaggerate: that perfect Christian family above simply doesn't exist – and really we never thought it did. Nevertheless, how many of us secretly believe that the other families in church are better at being Christians than us? Do we think their kids are somehow more teach-able, and the married couples more loving and forgiving than we are?

The truth is that real life is messy. There will be times when kids are tired, when work is stressful, when the house is a mess, and there's a mountain of washing that needs doing. There may be the odd occasion when family devotions *do* work, but in some homes, this kind of thing is never going to happen.

The vital thing to take hold of is that there is no *one* way of doing faith in the home. It's about finding what works best for you as a family.

'It's never too late to start doing something about faith in the home.'

We may be new to the whole concept of faith in the home. We may have come to faith recently, so don't know what to do or expect. We may have been Christians for a while, but not realised just what an opportunity we have with our kids. Or we may have been doing it for years. Whatever our situation, we need to remember that as their parents or carers, we are the most important people in our child's life, and it's never too late to start doing something about faith in the home. We'll explore some of the things that we can do in this section.

Andy

'As their parents or carers, we are the most important people in our child's life.'

Starting with me

KATHARINE

One of my favourite passages in the Bible is John 15. Jesus has gathered his disciples together. He knows what is ahead; within hours, he will be arrested and handed over to be crucified. He could have spoken to the disciples about anything, but he chose to speak to them about what it means to 'abide in him' – to live our lives in a close relationship with him.

'I am the vine; you are the branches. Whoever abides in me and I in him, he it is that bears much fruit, for apart from me you can do nothing' (John 15:5, ESV).

The word *abide* is mentioned ten times in John's record of this conversation, and when Jesus says something that often it is wise to take notice! To *abide with* someone means to *remain with* them or *to set up home with* them. So Jesus encourages us, as he did his disciples, to live in such a way that our hearts are connected to God all day long.

If we are to help our children on their faith journey, our starting point is here: to have a close relationship with God ourselves. We can't pass on what we don't have, but as we journey in our own relationship with God – abiding in him – our faith will spill over into our home. But

'If we are to help our children on their faith journey, our starting point is here: to have a close relationship with God ourselves.'

this kind of living doesn't just happen; we need to be intentional about putting it into practice. And it will look different in the different seasons of family life.

PATTERNS NOT PADLOCKS

I grew up on the practice of 'The Daily Quiet Time'. Each morning, I would try to take time to read the Bible and to pray. It was as natural to me as cleaning my teeth, and I couldn't imagine not doing it. That is, until 3 September 1988 when son #1, George Thomas Hill, made his appearance. Any thoughts of regular, ordered, quiet times went out of the window. My greatest achievement was to get dressed before lunchtime!

There are times in family life when we need to give ourselves some slack, and it was a while before I was able to find a different prayer and Bible reading routine that worked for me. Spiritual disciplines are important, but they need to be patterns not padlocks, in line with our personality as well as our season of life. What works for an introvert dad with school-age children will look entirely different to what works for an extrovert mum of pre-school triplets. Rather than struggle to do something that is just impossible in our situation, we can try to find a practice and a rhythm that works for us: one that is life-giving.

Practising the presence of God

Connecting with our Father in the busyness of everyday life

When I was up to my ears in nappies and pureed baby food, I came across a wonderful book called *The Practice of the Presence of God*. It was written by Brother Lawrence, a 15th-century monk. Brother Lawrence was a humble cook in a monastic community who had learned the art of being aware of God's presence and connecting with him through whatever he was doing – even washing the dishes. In that particular season of life, I found I was spending a lot of time washing dishes, and I tried to put some of his thinking into practice. Although I might occasionally have been able to grab time alone, I discovered it was also possible to connect with God while waiting for the laptop to connect, changing nappies, supervising children at the park, or loading the washing machine. And when I returned to work outside the home, I found this principle worked just as well in the busyness of office life.

We are all different, and we can all find our own key to keeping our relationship with God fuelled in the particular season we are in. Introverts may need time alone, while extroverts enjoy being in God's presence with others. Do what works for you.

Our spiritual journey will also be a window to God for our children, so we can be transparent in letting them see us praying, worshipping and reading the Bible. They need to see that our faith is authentic.

When our children were little, I began meeting up with three other mums. We would have coffee and talk about what was going on in our lives, and then one of us would look after the children while the other three prayed together. It wasn't perfect, but it gave us much needed support and friendship. In addition, our children were able to see what it meant to us to come to our Father with all our needs and requests. Our children have now all left home, but the four of us still meet to pray and it's a very precious time. Praying informally aloud may not be your style, but the principle is to find ways of keeping our relationship with God strong that work for us.

'We are the main spiritual influence in our children's lives.'

As parents, we are the main spiritual influence in our children's lives. And as we discover more about what it means to 'abide in him', we have an amazing opportunity on the rollercoaster ride of family life to model to them what seeking to live in a real relationship with God actually looks like.

Making visible the invisible

Showing our children what our relationship with God is like

ANDY

Our walk with God can be quite hard for our children to understand. We might pray silently in our heads, or we might read the Bible before they get up or when they are in bed. If we have 'quiet times', for example, what do our children understand by that? It can be mystifying for them, particularly when we lock ourselves away in our room for 20 minutes.

It's important to do what we can to make visible what is essentially invisible – to help our children see what our relationship with God is like. Rachel Turner, the author of *Parenting Children for a Life of Faith*, has particularly inspired me when it comes to creating ways for my children to see my walk with God. Recognising that kids are naturally very curious, she recommends that if we are spending some time with God in our bedroom, we might like to purposefully leave the door ajar so that they can peek inside. Or perhaps, as our kids get older, if we've been reading the Bible we might like to leave it out on the table with any notes we've made so that our children can have a sneaky look.

Katharine told me about a memory she has from her childhood:

'I remember waking up in the night several times and going down an unlit corridor to go to the loo. It would feel quite scary in the dark, but I would pass my parents' bedroom and sometimes see the light on. When I glanced in once, I saw my father kneeling by his bed with his head in his hands, praying. It's an image I will never forget. Seeing my father come before God in prayer on his own made a lasting impression on me.'

I have become particularly intentional about a certain ritual after church. I have always asked my kids what they've been doing during Sunday school as it gives me an insight into what they are learning. But I've also started saying to them, 'And can I tell you what I learned this morning?' When I share this with them, it lets them know that I am still learning more about God, and this has sometimes led to us having a deeper conversation.

The other very practical thing that I've been doing is praying aloud more regularly. I'm often in the habit of praying short prayers in my head, whether it be for a friend who is having a tough time or a story on the news as I'm driving along, but saying these aloud more often will really help my children understand that my faith is not just about Sunday mornings.

These short prayers demonstrate that I can bring world matters to God, along with personal thanks and challenges. And what I've noticed is that my kids have started picking up on these short prayers and even praying themselves.

However we interact with God, whether it be through a regular devotional time or on a more ad hoc basis, we need to let our children see what our relationship with him is like, taking away some of the mystery about it.

ANDY

You are qualified!

As I said earlier on, I often feel underqualified as a parent. There are so many situations that I never see coming, and I have to think quickly on my feet to work out the best plan of action. When it comes to nurturing faith in our children, we can also feel that we are just not qualified enough, many nagging thoughts robbing us of the privilege of helping our kids explore their relationship with God.

Some of us may have a past that we are not so proud of. We may have made some poor decisions or be very aware of our failings in the present. Perhaps our kids see us arguing and losing our temper. At times – such as when I've just shouted at my kids for not getting into their pyjamas after having told them to do so for the fifteenth time! – I'm so aware that I'm not sure that Jesus would have reacted in such a way. And we can so easily think that our past or our present failings or lifestyle prohibits us from the noble task of passing on the baton of faith.

Perhaps for some of us, the problem isn't about our lifestyle but about our intellectual knowledge. We feel that we can't help disciple our kids because we simply don't know enough – it should be left to those who have a robust understanding of Scripture and ideally a degree in theology! There are times I've been caught off guard by my five-year-old when she has sprung complicated questions on me about the Trinity or about other faiths.

WE DON'T HAVE TO BE THE PERFECT CHRISTIAN

The truth is that none of us fully has it all together. We all live with things in the past that we are not proud of, and we all continue to make mistakes in the present. As parents, most of us will find ourselves out of our depth when trying to explain difficult theological concepts to our children, especially ones that we might not understand ourselves!

But here's the thing: God has entrusted his children into our care, and he knew what he was doing! We are perfectly placed. Although we aren't able to live out our faith perfectly or anywhere near as well as we'd like to, and although we may not be fully able to explain every aspect of our faith and give our child all the answers, we *can* love our child and help them see that God loves us. We don't have to be perfect. We can use our mistakes as well as our successes to share with them how God is at work in us and what it means to be like Jesus. We can do this!

> ***'We can use our mistakes as well as our successes to share with our children how God is at work in us.'***

Being intentional

Looking for the little opportunities ...

I remember the first time we hosted my daughter's class for a birthday party. Thirty three- and four-year-olds excitedly poured into the church hall dressed up in their party gear. The noise was deafening, and I had committed to entertain all these children for 90 minutes. I felt completely overwhelmed and uncertain about how to get this off the ground.

It might be that you are feeling rather overwhelmed as you read this book. There are so many ideas about nurturing faith and you might be unsure where to begin – the task is just too daunting. But if you are starting the journey of passing on faith in the home for the first time, one thing that will really help is to be *intentional*. We need to be both purposeful and deliberate about what we're doing.

When I first began to get involved with the Kitchen Table Project (see p. 108), I had this light-bulb moment as to my role in nurturing faith in my kids. I'd done lots of youth work with older children, but I think I'd minimised how much impact could be made in children's early years. What's interesting –

and encouraging – is that as I got involved in this project, I realised that I was already doing lots of things naturally. For example, I was showing something of God's character just by being a loving parent, and I was already saying prayers with my kids when I put them to bed. The challenge for me was intentionally looking for more opportunities to nurture their faith every day.

A good way to start is by thinking through the rhythm of your day and week and then to look for the opportunities that are present. For example, if you take your toddler to nursery each morning, could you talk about God the Creator as you walk past and marvel at the trees? Or if you have a family meal together once or twice a week, could you say grace creatively, perhaps praying for the countries where your food originates or taking it in turns to say a phrase each?

START SMALL

When you are starting to be more intentional about passing on your faith, don't try to change everything at once; look instead for the little wins that you can make. Start small. It might even be that you begin with just one commitment, like praying before mealtimes. From that starting point, you'll see where things develop.

'Don't try to change everything at once; look instead for the little wins that you can make.'

If our children are already six, seven, or older, it's natural that it might feel a bit awkward to start something new like praying at bedtime or saying grace – perhaps we might feel that we've missed the boat! But we can be encouraged because the fact is that children are used to changes: routines alter, they go to new schools and activities, they may start staying up later at night as they get older, they start to get pocket money. If we explain to them that 'This is something we want to start doing as a family now' they will probably accept it more readily than you expect!

KEEPING ON TRACK

An important thing I've discovered is the power of accountability. I've been sharing with my wider family and other parents what I am doing to try to help my kids deepen their faith. And I have gone further than that: I have asked them to question me about how it's going from time to time to keep me being intentional about this.

We hope that you're feeling inspired to help your children explore faith as you read this book, but be prepared for that passion to lessen a bit; it can quickly fade, especially when life gets hectic or it appears that your efforts are not proving successful. To keep me on track, I have a fridge magnet with the verse from Deuteronomy 6 written on it. It reminds me about writing God's commandments on our hearts, getting them inside us, and then getting them inside our children:

'Talk about them wherever you are, sitting at home or walking in the street; talk about them from the time you get up in the morning to when you fall into bed at night' (Deuteronomy 6:6–9, The Message).

For me, talking about this priority with other Christian parents has meant that it hasn't fallen by the wayside.

Turning mistakes into opportunities

ANDY

It was embarrassing. I had agreed to take my two kids to see a show, and it wasn't until I got to the door that I realised it was for children aged over four. One of mine was only three. If we couldn't see the show, I could envisage a desperately upset five-year-old and a three-year-old having a massive tantrum. So I lied. When the lady on the door asked how old my three-year-old was, I confidently said she was four and just a little small for her age.

It was at that point that my five-year-old exclaimed, 'Daddy! She's three! She's not four. That's a lie.' The woman at the door looked at me with a disappointed expression, and I wanted the ground to swallow me up.

Our kids watch our lives intently. They pick up on the things we do and the things we say. Lots of that will be really positive, but the challenge is that they will always spot inconsistencies. I insist my children always tell the truth, and in that moment I had told a blatant lie right in front of them.

We all mess up (and maybe our kids see it more than anyone!), but our failures shouldn't stop us from helping our children develop a faith in Jesus. In fact, the way we respond when we have made mistakes can help them to learn about our faith.

'There will be times when we need to ask our children to forgive us for getting things wrong.'

We need to let our kids know that we are not perfect and that we need forgiveness. Talking through our mistakes and exploring the consequences of our failings allows our children to see the impact of sin. There will be times when we need to ask our children to forgive us for getting things wrong and for failing to live up to the standards we set. It's in these moments that we model the importance of conviction, humility and forgiveness. We demonstrate what reconciliation looks like and ultimately we give our children a picture of grace.

It's actually our mistakes and not our successes that give us an opportunity to talk poignantly about Jesus and the meaning of grace. Author Philip Yancey defines it beautifully: 'Grace is heartfelt, tinged with love, a spillover gift of the God who extended undeserved favour toward us.' In our failings, we can give our children a glimpse of what God's undeserved favour looks like.

The danger with our mistakes and failings is when we don't own up to them and try either to justify them or brush them under the carpet. When we do this, we see the Christian faith as no more than behaviour management. But it's not simply about following a list of rules and regulations. Christianity is about living life in response to what God has done for us on the cross. So if we try to cover up our mistakes and don't turn to God to confess and receive his forgiveness, we are failing to really unpack what grace looks like to our children. There is a danger that they will grow up thinking that being a Christian is simply about outward behaviour and living up to a Christian standard. And when they fail to live up to this standard later in life, they can simply not recognise the forgiveness that Christ offers.

'Let's not allow busyness to steal the time God designed us to have with our children.'

Innovation Photography

KATHARINE

The basic ingredient: time

Ask any parent of young children how they are doing and *busy* will almost certainly be one of the words they use in reply. We may be juggling school runs, doctors appointments, football training, swimming lessons, Cubs, Brownies, playdates, spelling, sums, holiday clubs, church activities, food shopping, fixing the car, paying the bills, cleaning out the guinea pig, walking the dog, washing, ironing (if absolutely necessary), and more besides. Our 24/7 always-on digital culture adds to the pressure as we text, tweet, and catch up on emails. If we are working outside the home, there will be the pressure of navigating work and childcare. If we are parenting together, we'll want time to invest in our relationship with our partner. And if we are parenting alone, we'll have all this to do with just one pair of hands. It's as if we are on a fast-moving conveyor belt and the last thing we need is *another* set of things we have to do – things like helping our children to grow in faith.

The good news is that while we need to be intentional about this, adding another set of jobs to an already stretched schedule is *not* what it's about.

CREATING SOME SPACE

That being said, there will be some of us whose commitments have got out of hand, and we may need to make some tough (but ultimately life-giving) choices. When our children were little, Richard and I had somehow got on the treadmill of endless after-school clubs and activities, all of which seemed to involve driving across town with hungry and fractious children in rush hour traffic. It wasn't something we'd chosen to do – it was more a way of life we'd drifted into. But one summer, we heard a talk by pastor Mike Breen called 'Rhythms of Life'. He spoke about taking our example from Jesus and encouraged us to deliberately create a family culture where we worked from a place of rest and had time – time to spend together, time just to be. It was a watershed moment. We came home and cleared the diary (not the most popular move!). And we decided that to create some space in the week, we would restrict the number of activities we did to ones that we could get to easily without having to make a mad dash across town. It was the best decision ever and set a rhythm of life in our family that we have benefitted from ever since.

As parents, God calls us to actively create a spiritual influence in the home that will shape our children's lives and their experiences of God. If we are going to be able to do that, the basic ingredient is time.

SEIZE TIME

First, we can *seize* time. We can take opportunities that are hiding in the nooks and crannies of the day to connect with our children – at bath time, bedtime, story time, meal times, on the school run, in the queue at Sainsbury's, or waiting for a sibling to come out of school. Rather than checking our email or texting a friend, we can make the most of these chances to connect with our children, developing a pattern of involvement in their lives.

MAKE TIME

As well as taking advantage of odd moments, we can also *make* time, purposely scheduling it in with our children. With busy lives and four children quite close together in age, Richard and I found when they were young that it was difficult for us to have any one-to-one time with them, so we began a little routine when one of us would take one of them to Tesco for breakfast on a Saturday morning. The children would take it in turns and the deal was that they could choose which of us they wanted to go with.

All went well, until I began to realise that I didn't often get to go; Richard seemed to be the companion of choice. Most of us are more insecure than we would like to admit, and I began to wonder why the children didn't want to go with me. Was I just not a fun mummy? Further questioning revealed the truth. When *I* took them for breakfast, we had Weetabix, wholemeal toast, fruit smoothies or bananas. When *Richard* was in charge, breaking all the rules, they had chocolate eclairs, Cheesy Wotsits and Coca Cola! I realised in that moment that as important as healthy eating is, this wasn't about five-a-day. The outing never was about the breakfast; it was simply about making time to connect together in the midst of the busyness of family life. The conversations we had were about football stickers, glitter pens or the next-door neighbour's new puppies – generally not anything significant. But every now and then we'd have a moment just to talk about the bigger issues of life, or to sow values in their hearts and ultimately point them to the God who made them.

Whatever the rhythm of our family is like, we can all find opportunities to spend some time together. It doesn't have to be expensive, and it doesn't have to be complicated. Let's not allow busyness to steal the time God designed us to have with our children.

Doubts and questions

ANDY

We don't need to have all the answers

We were just in the process of putting the kids to bed when we had the call that our friend had gone into labour early. The premature baby was struggling, and our friend had asked the church to pray. So as we sat on the edge of the bed with our children, we invited them to pray for this fragile little life. We prayed for God's healing.

The next day we had the news that the baby had not made it, and when our kids asked, we had to tell them the sad truth that the baby had died. The question quickly followed: 'Why didn't God heal the baby, Daddy?'

It's at moments like that when we face the reality that things don't always work out the way we'd like them to. Prayer is not simply a slot machine from which we get exactly what we ask for. I have been following Jesus for 20 years now and there are still times when I question why God allows such suffering.

'Why didn't God heal the baby, Daddy?'

In Scripture, and particularly in the psalms, we see that many great leaders doubted and wrestled with God. It's not wrong to go through experiences like these; the challenge is what we *do* with our doubts and questions. How much do we expose our children to the things that we wrestle with?

I believe that we need to create space for our children to explore difficult issues and to vocalise some of the doubts they have. When our children ask tricky questions, the default reaction can be to shut them down quickly, saying something along the lines of, 'Well, this is just what we believe' or 'That's what the Bible says.'

An alternative response, one which creates room for a deeper conversation, is to ask, 'What do you think?' and 'Why?' So rather than jumping in with the 'correct' theological answer (if we know it!), we can allow our children to think through what they believe and then offer our perspective afterwards.

Of course, if we do create space for this kind of conversation, at times our children might well ask us questions that we can't answer. So it's important to realise here and now that not only do we not have all the answers, but more than that – we don't *have* to have all the answers. We can choose, perhaps, to say something along the lines of, 'This is what I do know, but here are some of the questions I still have.' With older children especially, it might even be that you go on a journey together – for example, if you are looking at the topic of suffering, you might choose to watch a YouTube video giving a Christian apologetic or read a chapter of a book together and then talk about it. The main thing is that we give our children permission to articulate their questions and explore the issues.

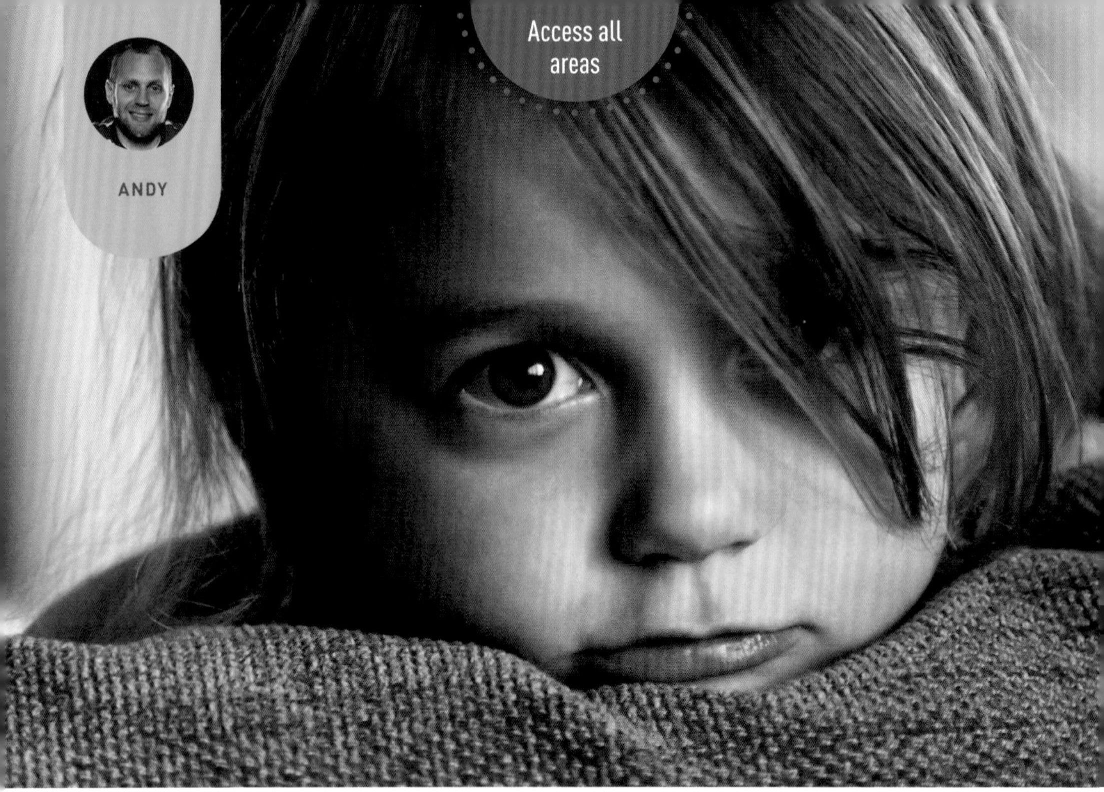

ANDY

Dealing with disappointment

Children have many different hopes and expectations for their lives – sporting ambitions, creative enterprises, dreams about having their own family. When their faith is developing, they will also have certain expectations about what a relationship with God is like. An important issue to bear in mind is that, like us, they will experience disappointment.

In his book *Getting Your Kids Through Church Without Them Ending Up Hating God*, Rob Parsons has written about three major disappointments that children will have as they grow up in the faith.

1 DISAPPOINTMENT WITH OTHERS

Youth workers, Christian friends and church leaders will make mistakes and fail to live up to God's standard. These 'falls from grace' can be really hard for children to understand and can lead to them questioning their own faith. When I wrote about this in a book called *Losing Faith* a few years ago, I interviewed people who had lost their faith. Time and time again, they shared how they had seen church leaders screw up and how detrimental that had been to their faith.

2 DISAPPOINTMENT WITH THEMSELVES

Children may make certain commitments in the early years, but when they make poor decisions in their teens at a party or with their friends, they can be wracked with guilt and disappointed with themselves. I have seen this particularly with young people who make great commitments for Christ at summer camps and then find they are falling back into bad decisions when they return to school.

3 DISAPPOINTMENT WITH GOD

From teenagers who have ardently prayed for a friend who has died of cancer to toddlers who ask Jesus for a longed-for toy at Christmas that isn't in the shops because it sold out months ago, our children will experience disappointment with God. Rob Parsons tells a story about a little girl who prays desperately for her sick goldfish to get better. Her mum, having put her to bed, heads downstairs to find that the goldfish is already dead. As she thinks about the tears to come and the inevitable questions about why God should let this happen, she's desperate to avert the grief and forestall any doubts her little girl might have about a good God. With the best of intentions, she heads out to Pet World, searches for a look-alike goldfish in the aquarium and races home to deposit it in the empty bowl.

The next morning her daughter rushes straight to the goldfish bowl and peers in: 'Mummy, he's done it! God's made Goldie well. And he's even made him fatter!'

That mum meant well and I, for one, can certainly identify with her. But if we want our child to develop a faith that lasts, we have an even greater responsibility than making life right for them. As Rob says, 'We have to prepare them for a truly terrifying moment. It is terrifying because, until that moment comes, God has never let them down. He has made Daddy's cough better and provided a sunny day for the birthday party; he has blessed thousands of people all across the world and always answered our prayers to guard us while we sleep. We have to get them ready for the day when they are disappointed with God.'

> *'We have to get them ready for the day when they are disappointed with God.'*

Part of equipping our children for these disappointments will happen as we open up about how we have been let down by people ourselves, share our failings, and talk about the mystery of a God who doesn't always heal our goldfish.

My dad died before my kids were born and so they often ask me questions about their grandad who they will never get to meet this side of heaven. The first time they asked me about him, I began to tear up, and I found myself explaining that there will be times when God doesn't always do what *we* think is best, but that even in those tough times we can be absolutely certain of his love, knowing that he wants to be with us and comfort us.

Part 4

The bigger picture

'We are not made to be isolated as human beings, but to be in relationship with each other.'

After school on Wednesdays was always a special time for one of our children. It was the day when one of the junior church leaders would meet him after school and take him to a local cafe for a hot chocolate usually laden with cream marshmallows and chocolate sprinkles! While the sugar rush was always welcome after a busy day at school, what was most precious about this time was the conversations they would have not just about our son's school day but about faith and, in particular, how they had seen God at work in their lives that week. Something that Richard and I have always prayed for our children since they were very small is that at the right time God would put people across their paths who would be an influence for good and point them to Jesus. This young man, who we had come to know and trust, was an answer to that prayer. Our son is now grown up, but I know that he (and we) are grateful for that relationship and for the seeds of faith that were sown in those after-school chats.

The famous opening line of a poem by John Donne says: 'No man is an island, entire of itself; every man is a piece of the continent, a part of the main ...' and the Bible bears this out when it says that we are all part of one body. We are not made to be isolated as human beings, but to be in relationship with each other, and the place in which this is most evident is the family. Whatever the shape or size of our family, and whatever unique opportunities or challenges come our way, our family relationships are worth investing in.

Katharine

Invest in your relationship

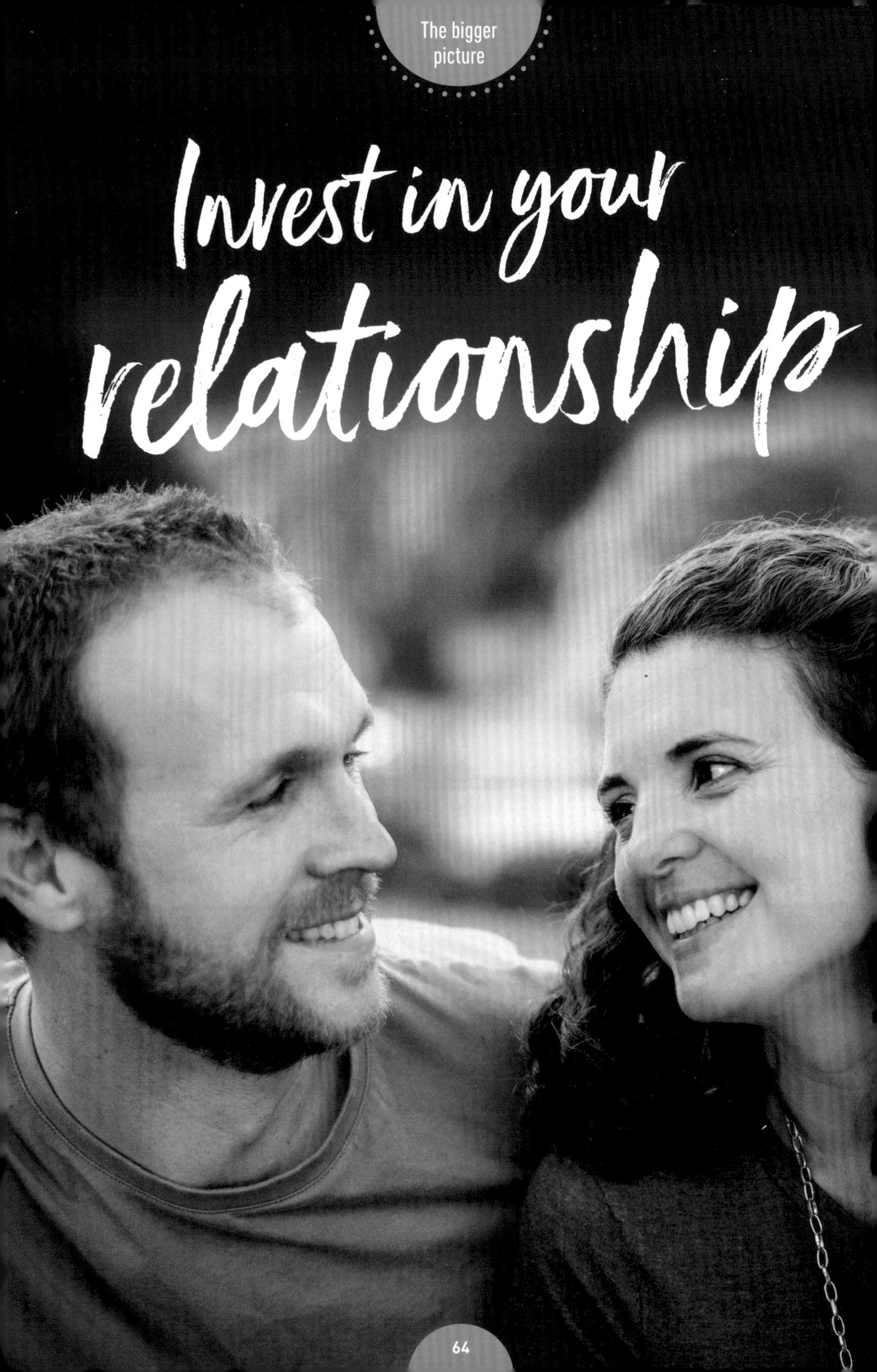

We will all be familiar with the aircraft safety announcement that tells adults to put their oxygen mask on first before attending to their children. It sounds counter-intuitive but on reflection makes perfect sense. And as parents, we need to make sure we are looking after ourselves well enough to have the energy and resources to take care of our children. An important part of that will be giving time to the significant adult relationships in our lives. If we are parenting alone, this will be relationships with friends, and if we are married, our marriage relationship.

From my work at Care for the Family and previously as a family solicitor, I know all too well the painful truth that it isn't always possible or sometimes even desirable to keep every marriage together. Having said that, if we are married, one of the best things that we can do for our children is to invest in our couple relationship.

While there are always exceptions to the rule, a large body of research shows that children do best in life when they grow up with parents who are committed to each other and are prepared to work through the highs and lows of their relationship together. A marriage relationship like this is a secure foundation for children and models relationship skills – how to talk and listen, disagree and find joint solutions, apologise and forgive, and give unconditional love and commitment.

PUT ON LOVE

One of the things Richard and I love doing is helping engaged couples prepare for marriage. We spent time with one such couple last night. They came in holding hands, and as they sat down she moved her chair towards him so they could be close. He couldn't take his eyes off her. You could feel the love in the room! We encouraged them to enjoy this time in their lives but also explained that it may not always feel like this. There would be days ahead when they won't feel in love – days when they will have to *choose* to keep love alive. In Colossians 3:16, a passage sometimes read at weddings, the apostle Paul urges his readers to 'Put on love'. It's as if he is speaking of putting on a jacket in the morning. Love is a choice.

There are many ways we can choose to put on love in our marriages. It takes intention, it takes effort, and it takes time. But if we are prepared to work at it, it will benefit not only us and our relationship together, but our children as well.

When our children were little, Richard suggested we ask friends to look after our brood so we could go away for a night, just the two of us. He wanted 24 hours when we could step off the treadmill of family responsibilities, pause, have fun, and remember what it was that attracted us to each other in the first place! I declined. I thought we'd be neglecting our children in some way by abandoning them and going away. Looking back, I realise I was wrong in that.

At about the same time, we were encouraged to put a regular 'date night' in the diary. It could be a drink at the local pub, a walk on a sunny (or rainy!) evening, a coffee out, or a night in at home on our own together with a ban on emails, ironing, social media and DIY. Having this planned time together is consistently one of the most important things we do to build our marriage. It's not always wonderfully romantic, but the regularity of it has woven itself into the fabric of our marriage over the course of time.

WHEN OUR PARTNER DOESN'T SHARE OUR FAITH

If our spouse shares our faith, there are a couple of specific things we can do to keep our marriage strong and keep God at the centre. But, first, a word to those of us who are married to someone who does not share our faith. This can be a challenging situation, but the truth is that simply by building up our marriage, we are providing our children with a warm, secure foundation for their lives. These things are never easy, but where possible we can try to be honest with our spouse about what our faith means to us and about our desire to give our children every opportunity to follow Jesus for themselves. We can try not to make faith a battleground, but we can gather others to support and pray for us on the journey.

'If we are married, one of the best things that we can do for our children is to invest in our couple relationship.'

PRAYING TOGETHER

One specific way we can build intimacy in our relationship if our spouse shares our faith is to learn to pray together. Richard and I didn't do this when we were first married as it felt awkward and we didn't know how to start. A wise friend encouraged us to begin by saying a short prayer for each other in the morning. Thirty years on, this routine has now become as familiar to us as getting dressed in the morning – we can't imagine starting the day without it. If it's something you've never done before, why not try making a start. Perhaps you could say the Lord's Prayer together or light a candle and pray in silence together – see what works for you. Praying together as a couple draws us closer to each other, closer to God, and models to our children that turning to our heavenly Father in prayer is a natural thing to do.

'Involve others in helping to keep your relationship strong.'

WORKING TOGETHER

Many couples have also found their relationship strengthened by serving together in some way. It may be by being on the coffee rota, helping at the food bank or the children's choir, opening their home or leading a small group – whatever is do-able according to their giftings and particular season of life. This is certainly not about allowing church busyness to encroach on family time. It involves finding a place where we can naturally exercise our gifts in a complementary way that helps builds our marriage, models service to our children, and helps keep God at the centre of our relationship.

SUPPORT FROM OTHERS

Finally, life can be hard and pressures come to every marriage, so involve others in helping to keep your relationship strong. For a number of years now, we have met with another couple once a fortnight on a Tuesday evening. We have a meal together, we share life experiences, often laugh together, sometimes cry together and always pray together. Most importantly, we make ourselves accountable to each other in our marriages. The writer to the Hebrews urges us to, 'Spur one another on towards love and good deeds' (Hebrews 10:24) and our friends have done this for us. They have encouraged us, cheered us on, and prevented us from slipping up on many an occasion – and we like to think that we have done the same for them.

While this has been an incredible source of support and friendship for us, there have been wider consequences. Little eyes are watching and little ears are listening. When our daughter was 11, she was helping me lay the table for our Tuesday meal with our friends and she looked up and said, 'Mummy, when I get married, I'm going to have friends that we can do this with.' She got married last year and I am hoping that she will do just that.

Keeping our couple relationship alive – choosing to love – will benefit not just our marriage but will have a lasting impact on our children as well.

Parenting alone

KATHARINE

Passing on faith as a single parent

At a recent Care for the Family event, a single parent mum came to see me in the break. She told me she had a strong faith, and her deepest desire was for her children to come to know and love Jesus as well. But she was fearful – fearful that she hadn't been a good role model and fearful that some of the issues she was facing were simply because she was parenting alone. I listened to her story, and while I knew there were no easy answers, I did know one thing. I reassured her that many of the challenges she was facing were nothing to do with the fact that she was parenting alone; they were simply issues that were common to every mum and dad. As she walked away, she looked back and smiled. I could almost see the weight fall from her shoulders. She simply needed to hear that the issues she was going through were normal.

And in the same way, the wisdom and principles in this book that encourage us to be intentional in nurturing our children's faith will apply whatever the shape or size of our family.

Having said that, there are some extra things to take into account for those parenting alone. Whatever our circumstances – perhaps we have been widowed or there has been relationship breakdown – life can be hard as a single parent. We are dealing with all the same issues and sometimes more, but with half the resources, and the challenge can be immense. While it is not one-size-fits-all, there are principles that many single parents have found helpful in seeking to pass on faith to their children.

GETTING SUPPORT FROM OTHERS

Sean, a single parent dad, speaks of the value of having friends in his church and, in particular, in his small group – other men who support and pray for him and mums who are able to offer wise counsel from a female perspective as his girls grow older. In the same way, many single parent mums are grateful to have dads they know and trust from church who will come alongside their children, not just to kick a football around but to talk on a deeper level about the bigger issues of life.

ACKNOWLEDGING DOUBTS, CONFUSION AND ANGER

In working with single parents over the years at Care for the Family, we have often been humbled by their resilience in the face of challenge and have heard many wonderful testimonies of God's faithfulness even in the darkest of times. I recently had the privilege of speaking to Ruth, whose husband had died leaving her with two young children. She spoke of having to trust God in the darkness not just for herself but for her children too. She recognised that she needed to allow them to work through their anger, bewilderment and doubt for themselves, all the while praying that they would know God as a loving Father, even when she was doubting it herself.

RECOGNISING THE POWER OF HONESTY

I was also moved by Sharon's story. She was married to a Christian and had two children. When they were quite young, she had an affair and the marriage broke down. She regretted her part in the divorce and felt a deep sense of shame, worrying for years about the effect it would have on her children's future life choices. As they grew older, instead of avoiding the issue, she discovered the power of speaking honestly to them about what had happened, admitting her mistakes, and telling them how God had given her a new start.

There is a lovely verse in the book of Joel that says, 'I will repay you for the years the locusts have eaten' (Joel 2:25). While many single parents will have had a difficult journey, we can be encouraged that as we seek to share the reality of our faith walk with our children even in the most challenging of times, God's desire will be to draw them to himself.

TRUSTING OUR CHILDREN TO GOD WHEN THEIR OTHER PARENT DOESN'T BELIEVE

Maggie is a single parent and mother of two. Her husband went from being a believer to walking away from the family and from faith. When he began living a lifestyle that was opposed to the values she wanted the children to grow up with, she found it very difficult to deal with:

'It's hard when you are the only Christian parental influence in their lives, but I have learned not to put pressure on myself and to trust my children to God. I have tried to live out my faith in the everyday ups and downs of family life, and I hope and pray that my children will notice the difference that intentionally inviting Jesus into our home makes. I have also tried not to run down my ex-husband in front of the children. Whatever his life choices, he is still their dad, and I need to allow them to make up their own minds about what they choose to believe.'

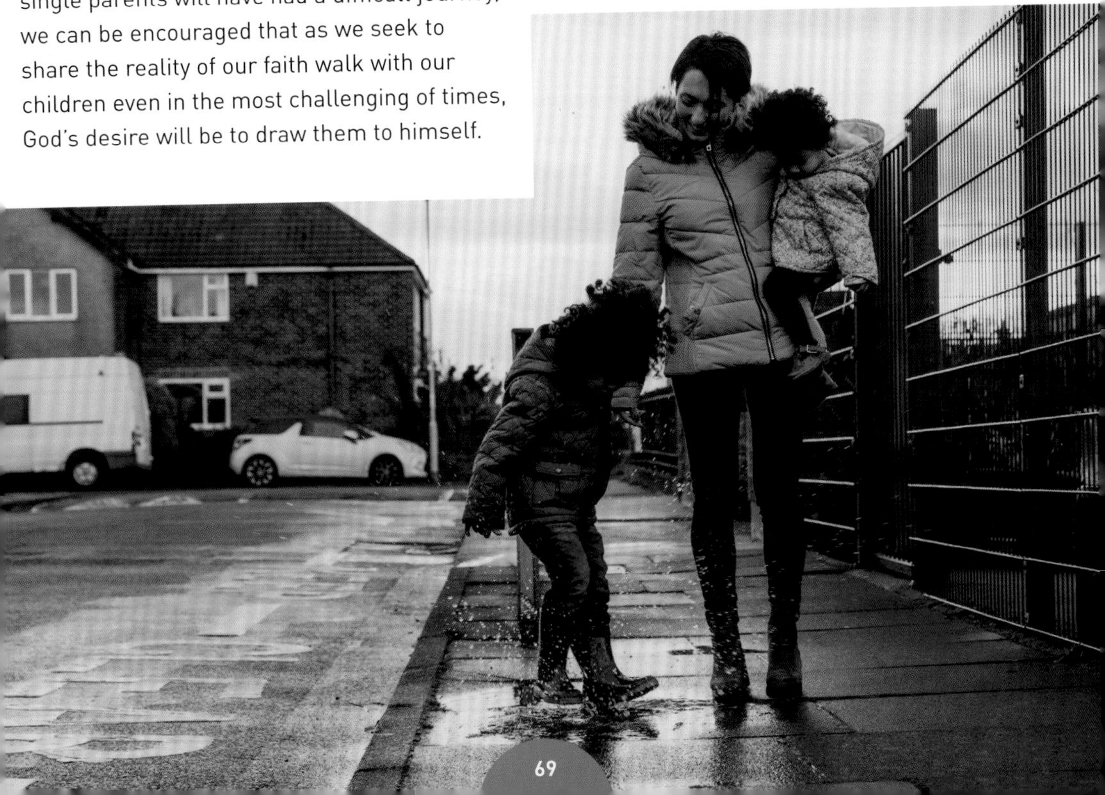

Innovation Photography

Parenting from a distance

KATHARINE

Making the most of the time we have with our kids

John watched out of the window until the tail lights of the car disappeared from view. He stayed looking out for a few more minutes as his mind went over the events of the last year. In the early days, their marriage had been happy, but somewhere between their daughter's first tooth and their son's first day at school they had lost each other. And now they were separated, and he was living on his own, ten miles from his beloved children. If he was honest, he felt a failure as a dad.

John's situation is not unusual. Many mums and dads living away from their children's family home are trying to give the task of parenting their very best shot and, for Christian parents, trying to work out how to sow seeds of faith at a distance. So far in this book, we have focussed on the importance of building a secure, warm relationship with our children as being the best greenhouse for those seeds to germinate. Undoubtedly, there will be painful situations when the circumstances of relationship breakdown mean that this is not possible. However, even if we are not with our children seven days a week, we will usually still have opportunities to play our part in influencing their lives.

STAYING IN REGULAR CONTACT

Keeping in close contact with our children strengthens our relationship and builds trust. If we are parenting at a distance, it will be important to make sure we have school plays, parents' evenings, football matches etc. in our calendar. Distance may mean that it isn't possible to attend them all, but if that's the case, we can continue to show an interest, asking how the event went. And we can make full use of digital technology – for example, communicating across the miles with Facetime to catch up on our child's day or reading a story and saying bedtime prayers together on Skype.

PLANNED VISITS

We may already have regular arrangements firmly in place, but if not, take time to plan these so that everyone knows what is happening. Agreeing and keeping to times is so important and is a way of building trust in our children's lives.

STRUCTURE

Children do best when they know what to expect, so trying to keep to existing routines regarding meal times, screen times, homework, bedtime and so on is important. This will help make the transition from one house to the other as smooth as possible. Giving our children their own room when they stay with us (if that's possible), or even giving them their own things – such as a blanket or cup, conveys to them the message that they belong in and have a special place in our home.

TRADITIONS

We've already talked about the value of family traditions (those 'We always ...' things) in giving children a sense of belonging and creating strong memories to look back on. We can also keep up with the traditions we already have and introduce some new ones as they naturally occur. They don't have to be expensive, just things that we do regularly on certain days or at certain times of the year. It might be sitting down together with a drink and biscuit when they arrive at our house, playing a particular game in the evening, putting up a special banner on birthdays, or going to the same place for brunch on Saturdays.

CHURCH INVOLVEMENT

If our child is with us for the weekend and we are involved in our local church, there is the opportunity to take them along. Joining in the age-appropriate groups and activities and getting to know children the same age will help them feel they belong. If our child's other parent has an active faith it may be that they will have two opportunities to be involved in the family of God.

When we are parenting at a distance, we may not have as much contact with our children as we would like, and we will have to work a little harder at building the relationship. However, we can focus on the quality of our time with them rather than the quantity, letting them know how much we love spending time with them and seizing every chance we have to be together. Even if we are not around them 24/7, there are still many opportunities to be an influence in their lives.

The gift of grandparents

Modelling faith and sowing wisdom and values in children's lives

KATHARINE

Research has shown that one of the key elements in passing on faith to the next generation is the support of members of the wider family – especially grandparents.

Many grandparents today are light years away from the traditional images in children's storybooks of little old ladies sitting in a rocking chair by an open fire with their knitting or kindly older gentlemen in horn-rimmed glasses smoking a pipe and reading the paper. Today's grandparents may be business entrepreneurs, go hang-gliding and mountain biking, hang out at music festivals, do Pilates and swing kettlebells, or have busy jobs as CEOs of companies and hundreds of followers on social media.

Some live down the road and some are miles away from their children and grandchildren. Some are full-time carers for grateful parents trying to juggle the demands of work and childcare. Some are living with the pain of the breakdown of their child's relationship. But whatever their family situation, grandparents can have a wonderful influence on the lives of their grandchildren and can, in particular, play a vital role in encouraging their faith.

In the relentless busyness of family life, although it's not always possible, grandparents can often be the ones who are able to give children the precious gift of time. They can read a story without skipping a page, pause to watch a caterpillar climb up a leaf, patiently untangle knotted hair after swimming, and answer the endless

'One of the key elements in passing on faith to the next generation is the support of members of the wider family – especially grandparents.'

questions of 'Why?' One eight-year-old put it like this: 'Everyone should have a grandmother because they're the only grown ups that have time.'

The grandparent/grandchild relationship has been described by psychologists as 'an emotionally uncomplicated form of love'. Maybe this is to do with the fact that grandparents can have all the fun and opportunity for influence without bearing the ultimate responsibility for the children – they don't need to worry about making sure that spellings are learned and music practice is done. Whether it is an eight-year-old who has been left out of the team or a fifteen-year-old who has been the butt of a Facebook post, grandparents can give children reassurance, encouragement and wise advice over the years. They have it in their power to give their grandchildren an incredible gift: the reassurance that they are loved simply for who they are.

And grandparents can help a child think through some of the deepest questions of life – questions such as 'Who am I?' and 'Where do I belong?' A lovely African proverb says: 'When an old person dies, a library burns down.' My father is 100 years old and is an endless source of anecdotes. When they were growing up, my children never tired of hearing him talk about 'the old days' – how he rode through central London on a Fairy bike to school and when few houses had a bath and fewer still a telephone. They loved to hear about the tricks he got up to while growing up and what he did as a young man in the Second World War. Author Lois Wyse said, 'Grandparents connect the dots from generation to generation' and that's why these stories are precious.

As well as seizing opportunities in everyday life, there will also be times to be proactive in giving our parents the chance to share their faith with their grandchildren by visiting them or arranging for them to stay. When children see their grandparents living out an authentic faith that has stood the test of time, it will speak powerfully to them. Ask your parents to include your children in their own devotions, prayers, Bible reading and church activities.

Not all children have grandparents who are alive (I didn't know mine), and if there are family difficulties, grandparent/grandchild relationships can be complex. Our children's grandparents may not share our faith, but in situations like these, the wider family and friends can step in. We can intentionally include aunts, uncles, godparents, neighbours and friends in our children's lives, enabling them to play an important role in coming alongside our children to model faith and sow wisdom and values.

When one of our children was quite young, he was invited to spend half-term with his best friend Zac – but with Zac's grandparents. They lived some distance away, and we arranged to rendezvous halfway there in a McDonald's. As part of the handover, I treated the boys to a Happy Meal. Excitingly, it came in a box covered with a space images and the most mind-blowing facts and figures about the solar system. Little eyes grew wide as Zac's Grandpa read these out to the boys: billions and billions of stars make up the Milky Way; the furthest star we can see is 4,000 light years away; there is a supergiant star over 100,000 times more luminous than our sun and so on. Suddenly, part way through, this wonderful grandpa paused and said in the most natural of ways, 'And, boys, do you know that in the Bible there is a little verse which says, "And [God] also made the stars"? Isn't he amazing! ... Now how are those chips?'

At that moment, I was so grateful for this wise grandfather who had gently just made a precious deposit in a five-year-old boy's life. It's a moment I won't easily forget.

ANDY

Making the most of our church family

The Church! It's a bold concept! God crafts us together from different generations, races and cultures to be a new society that represents him. So let's take advantage of the myriad giftings, jobs, ages, backgrounds and experience of those who make up the Church – it's a tremendous resource as we help our children develop faith.

Across different church traditions, there are a host of ways in which we try to encourage cross-generational engagement. One of the common ways is the role of godparents. Jo and I have the privilege of being godparents to four amazing kids. Initially, as you prepare for the service of dedication, the responsibility of the role is clear. The problem is that as the years pass by and situations change, we can easily lose sight of that responsibility, and often, being a godparent can end up involving little more than sending a birthday card once a year rather than investing into that child's spiritual life. As parents, it's helpful to look for ways to help our children's godparents in their role – for example, by making a note in our diary to email them once a quarter with an updated picture and some specific prayer requests.

Whether or not our kids have godparents, we need to work out how we can better tap into the rich resource of the Church. Again, we need to be proactive about this. We can't wait for people to rush over to help with nurturing our child's faith; we need to go out and invite them to be involved in this incredible opportunity.

We might consider inviting five people to

Tap into the rich resources of the Church. Proactively invite people to help nurture your child's faith.

commit themselves to supporting our child's faith journey. They might be a mix of ages, including a teenager and an elderly person. It's best to be clear about what we are expecting of them and why we are asking them to do this, and to explore with them how this relationship might work. For example, could they support our child on special occasions like birthdays or come over occasionally for a Sunday roast after church?

My friend has a great example of involving the wider church. Her daughter had been very excited about her forthcoming birthday when she would turn double figures, so my friend decided to mark this occasion by inviting some significant women around for a birthday tea. Aunties and grandmothers, the children's worker and the youth leader, the pastor and her daughter's teenage mentor were all included.

After the sandwiches and cake, the girl was presented with cards and letters to encourage her in her faith journey. Each woman took it in turn to read something to her that would encourage her, many mentioning and affirming the amazing qualities she has. They then followed this up by praying together for her. My friend and her daughter now regularly re-read the cards and letters, which are lovingly compiled in a scrapbook. That birthday tea was more important than the main party and the gifts because it was in that profound moment that this young girl discovered that the church community was with her and for her as she matured in her faith journey.

We can aim to build a strong relationship between our child and their supporters. We might stick photos of them on our child's wall, for example, and explain to our child that these people are regularly praying for them. And we can encourage our child to pray for them too, so that the relationship is two-way.

'It was in that profound moment that this young girl discovered that the church community was with her and for her.'

Lightstock

Innovation Photography

ANDY

Dad talk

When it comes to parenting, a danger with some of us men (though by no means all) is that we can let the mums take the lead. And in talking to friends who are fathers about nurturing faith in the home, I've noticed there is sometimes the sense that this responsibility also rests more on their wives' shoulders rather than theirs. But this book is about helping *parents* build faith in the family, not just mums. Where possible, both parents should jump into this opportunity!

It might be that you, as a dad, are out working longer hours and have less time with your kids, or it might be that mum is in this situation, but the truth is that *both* parents have a responsibility and commitment to your child's spiritual development that you can't ignore.

We are already teaching our children by example – through the way we are living our lives. The challenge is: *what* are we teaching? If we are modelling a life where our children only see our faith on a Sunday morning they will pick up on this. They will think that faith is not that important to us.

The old adage says, 'No one ever says on their deathbed: "I wish I'd spent more time in the office."' But I'm sure as well that no one on their deathbed says, 'I wish I'd spent more time on social media/finalising my fantasy football team/watching TV.'

NO ONE CAN REPLACE YOU AS YOUR CHILDREN'S FATHER

There are times after a long day of meetings and commuting when all I want to do is reach for the TV remote control, but the truth is that there is no one who can replace us as our children's father, and research shows just how powerful time spent with our kids can be. Depending on our situation, we may not be able to pick our kids up from school and talk about their day with them on the way home, we may miss bath time and bedtime, so it's easy to think that our child will naturally have deeper heart conversations with their mum. But this doesn't have to be true.

I believe we need to be *present* when we're with our kids. And when I say *present*, I mean that our phones are switched off or that we're not quickly trying to reply to our emails! We can be proactive about carving out some special one-to-one time with each of our children. We've already talked about this in respect of both parents, and it's especially important for dads who have less time with them than mum. I know some dads who go for a cooked breakfast on a Saturday morning with their kids, and I take my daughter to do parkrun before church on Sunday morning. It's on these mornings that I am able to talk very naturally about faith with her and give her words of encouragement that I pray will have a powerful impact for good in her life.

Parenting children with additional needs

KATHARINE

At Care for the Family, we have a wonderful initiative that supports and befriends parents of children with additional needs. Whatever the condition and however complex – whether it's a toddler with a rare syndrome, a child with little movement or who is unable to speak, or a pre-schooler with a condition still to be diagnosed – in addition to the usual trials and tribulations of parenting, these parents face challenges and experiences that can place huge pressure on the family.

One of our befrienders describes it like this: 'A family with an additional needs child is like any other family ... but with "extras".'

For that reason, when thinking through how best to help build faith in a child with additional needs, the very last thing their parents need is a list of extra things to do. Hopefully, it will come as a relief to discover that as with every family, one of the keys is to simply make faith a part of everyday life in the midst of the joys and the challenges.

Nicola Watson, who is Care for the Family's Additional Needs Support Coordinator, describes it like this:

'Paul wrote to the Corinthians saying, "Your very lives are a letter that anyone can read by just looking at you. Christ himself wrote it – not with ink, but with God's living Spirit; not chiselled into stone, but carved into human lives" (2 Corinthians 3:3, The Message). The wiping of all things mucky, the washing, the waiting, the lifting, the carrying, the grieving, the chivvying, the sleep deprivation, the email-writing, the phone calls, the hospital appointments, the therapies, the meetings with teachers, the

exclusions, the explanations, the fear, the fight ... all this and more. You are sharing and inspiring faith every day of your life.'

Beth, who runs a charity helping churches to set up cafe drop-in sessions for parents of children with additional needs, gives this advice to those she supports:

'Don't be tempted to water down faith. God is a perfect Father who has created our children in love. He wants to make himself known to them. Try not to get in the way or put a limit on what they can understand.'

Pippa is mum to Barney who has Down's syndrome. She writes:

'We let him see our faith as a normal part of our life. We talk about Jesus and pray together, letting Barney take the lead in praying if he wants to and talking about how we can help people because Jesus loves them. We do all the things we'd do normally in any other area of his life – we listen hard to understand his questions, praying for wisdom for the right way to respond. Barney's learning disability means he sees the world in black and white, which has led to some interesting moments. For example, as we've often talked about swearing or smoking not being a good thing to do, it is not unknown for him to see a stranger smoking or using bad language and to go and tell them off!

Barney is less inhibited than many of us in sharing his faith, and we have learned the power of giving him opportunities to do that. Our new church recently had a launch weekend, and Barney came with me to give out leaflets in our neighbourhood. It's a challenging area and it took me courage to do. We'd just about finished when Barney spotted some young guys hanging around a house further down the street. He said that he wanted to give a flyer to them. I started to say no because I was worried they'd be unkind to him and I wanted to protect him, but then I felt that nudge of the Holy Spirit and I let him go. When I arrived shortly afterwards, he was cheerfully and unselfconsciously inviting them to the church launch events. It was something that delighted me and must also have brought pleasure to the heart of God.'

'A family with an additional needs child is like any other family but with "extras".'

Pippa also spoke of the importance of discovering the unique way our child best connects with God.

'Barney can't read, but he loves music. Much of his understanding of faith comes from worship songs on CDs and YouTube. He listens, sings and drums. I make an effort to keep him supplied with new CDs that I think he would like. He genuinely worships and is often very moved during this time.'

When I asked Pippa what she would say if she could give just one piece of advice to those parenting children with additional needs, she said:

'We have learned much from Barney. Be willing to be humbled and always see your child through the eyes of heavenly wisdom. Remember that what matters to God is very different to what the world values (1 Corinthians 1:27).'

Wise words indeed.

Adoption and fostering

We have already looked at the different ways that parents of children with additional needs can seek to pass on faith. Depending on the circumstances, all those challenges and more can apply to adoptive parents and foster carers, particularly those opening their homes to children who have been damaged by poor attachments, early trauma or neglect. One small study found that 75% of children referred for adoption medicals had a history of prenatal alcohol exposure and were suffering from foetal alcohol syndrome as a result. Perhaps it is for this reason that parenting in these situations has been called 'parenting for marines'.

Sharing our faith with our children in these circumstances can also seem extra-tough. There may be challenges related to our child's sense of identity or belonging, their feelings about God as a Father, and what they understand about why God would allow difficult things to have happened to them.

Kelly and Mark have been fostering for eleven years, and some of the children have had really difficult backgrounds. Kelly writes:

'We try to be honest with the children in a gentle and appropriate way, explaining that wrong was done to them, and always reassuring them that they were not responsible for what happened. It can be helpful to acknowledge that bad things can happen to anyone, and that these experiences don't mean that God is absent or uncaring. Jesus was with them all the time and has never left them, even in the worst times. We like to explain that God is showing his love to them by providing this loving, safe family for them now.

We also do our best to make our home one where the children can experience prayer and the Bible as a natural part of everyday life. One thing we have come to understand is that the process of healing and wholeness is, most often, an ongoing journey (as it is for us all) rather than a one-time experience.'

Kelly also speaks about the value of being supported by others and being part of a healthy Christian community:

'They don't have to know all the details, but it's a wonderful help to have some people who will commit to praying for and supporting both you and the child on an ongoing basis.'

Elizabeth has a foster daughter aged one who she is in the process of adopting. Elizabeth comments:

'I make it my prayer that my daughter will know that she is loved by God and that she is precious to him. I want her to feel at home in his family and to know that God specialises in adoption! Whatever her questions about her past, I pray that she would find her sure identity in God.'

Pete and Isla are also foster carers. He says:

'We encourage our kids to share in a generous way, to forgive, to be kind and thoughtful etc. We say stuff like, "We are Taylors, and Taylors share the good things we have."'

For all of these families, the very act of fostering is itself a witness to their trust in God. In his book *Home for Good*, Krish Kandiah writes:

'I have met many people who have become Christians as a result of the love their foster parents or adoptive parents showed them. They didn't just hear the message of God's love, compassion and sacrifice for them, they experienced it through the care and unconditional love they received from their carers.'

We can be encouraged that God is passionate about caring for the 'widows and orphans' – for the vulnerable and those on the margins of family life. His desire is for them to feel secure in his love and to know him as the perfect Father.

Part 5

Putting it all into practice

'No two children are the same and each family has different ways of practising their faith.'

This final chapter is about practical things we can do to strengthen our children's relationship with God. The ideas are based around four key areas: prayer, Bible reading, habits and mission. Again, it's important to mention that there isn't *one* correct approach to nurturing faith in your child – no two children are the same and each family has different ways of practising their faith.

You have freedom to be flexible about what you do. You might find some of the ideas below easy to put into practice, but others might not work for you at all. Perhaps one of these suggestions will act as a springboard for your own unique ideas. You don't need to do everything at once, but as your child explores faith, you can pick and mix the ideas and adapt them for the different seasons of their life.

There will be times when faith activities go as planned – and there will be times when they don't and it all seems like very hard work! The key is to choose what best suits you and your family. Enjoy the opportunity to experiment, share stories with other parents, and keep on learning from your experiences.

Andy

Getty images

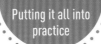

ANDY

Launch Pad

Giving our kids a framework and space to encounter God for themselves

When it comes to nurturing our kids' faith, it's vitally important that we keep the purpose in mind. It's not primarily about trying to get them to behave. And it's good to remember that we can't have their relationship with God for them. Ultimately, our vision is to give our child the opportunity to respond to God's love and get to know him personally for themselves.

There are two significant challenges here. The first is that nurturing faith can become solely about head knowledge. We can perhaps think that if our children know enough about it, they will automatically develop an authentic faith. However, an intellectual understanding of God is not enough; we want our children to have a *relationship* with him.

The second challenge is that sometimes we want to act as middlemen. We can be so fearful of our children walking away from God that we attempt to 'come through' for him. In the worst-case scenario, we end up manipulating situations rather than trusting God to be God. As tempting as it might be to put God in a good light by 'answering' our child's prayer (if we have the ability to do so), we shouldn't just fix things.

We don't have to over-explain God; there will always be some things that are mysterious about him – his ways are not always our ways. Allowing our child to foster a relationship with him is not about us explaining everything and doing everything on our terms. Instead, we can aim to give them the framework and space to connect with and encounter God themselves. It's about creating a launch pad for their faith journey.

Learning to pray

ANDY

When Jesus taught his disciples how to pray, he began with the words 'Our Father'. I find this really helpful to remember when praying: God is ultimately the Father of our whole family. It's important that we pray *for* our kids, but it's also vital to pray *with* our kids, so that we show them what it is like to have a relationship with God our Father – we can come to him with both the big things and the little things in our lives. It also demonstrates to them that our faith is about more than meeting together at church on a Sunday morning; it's about how we do life in the manic-ness of a Monday morning! Here are some ideas you might like to try to get your kids praying:

1

GIVING THANKS

Part of what praying is about is to thank God for who he is and what he has done. A great way of modelling thankfulness to our kids is to say grace – a simple pre-meal prayer. It might be that everyone thanks God for one thing before you all eat.

2

USING LITURGY – FORMAL PRAYERS

My daughter attends a Catholic primary school and loves some of the well-known prayers that are said. She once told me, 'Daddy, you just make your prayers up.' Try out this prayer as you make the sign of the cross: 'From my head to my heart, from shoulder to shoulder, I belong to you, Lord Jesus. Amen.'

Another little prayer I came across that I like to say as I kiss my kids good night is very short, but so rich in theology: 'Thank you, God, that you have given me your child to look after, to know and to love. Amen.'

3

CONVERSATIONAL PRAYER

I mentioned before how author Rachel Turner has inspired me, and she has written some brilliant material about praying with children and helping them talk with God naturally and conversationally. She suggests that you ask your child a question – something like, 'What was the best thing that happened today?' – and then invite them to tell God about it, either in silence or by whispering into their pillow.

We can explain to our children that they can simply 'chat' to God – they don't have to talk in special ways or use formal language when praying. Encourage them to talk to him about anything, large or small – for instance, telling him what their favourite film is or funny things such as whether they'd rather have an elephant or a bear as a pet! In doing this, we are creating space for them to build their own direct relationship with God.

Getty Images

4

LISTENING PRAYER

Prayer is not just about talking to God; it is about listening to him. Rachel Turner talks of 'chat and catch' as a way of thinking about prayer – 'catch' meaning that we are expecting God to talk back to us. We can tell our children that God might speak in all sorts of ways – maybe in our thoughts, through words, with pictures, through feelings, or as a sensation in our bodies.

When we pray about decisions that we need to make, it can be great to ask our kids, 'What do you think God might be asking us to do?' It highlights that we expect God to lead us.

5

TEAM TIME PRAYER

I have a friend who shouts, 'Team Time' before everyone leaves the house in the morning. They all gather in a huddle to say a short prayer for the day ahead. The other day, I heard about some siblings in their twenties who have left home but still automatically shout 'Team Time' before setting off on a journey or leaving to meet a difficult challenge that day.

Andres F Uran

6

LIGHTING A CANDLE

Words can often be hard to find when you or your child want to pray for a loved one who is ill or facing difficulties. A great way of helping them to participate in prayer at times like these is to invite them to light a candle with you and simply sit together to watch it burn for a moment. Encourage them that just as the candlelight flows out into the room, so God knows what is in our hearts, even if we don't know what to say to him in prayer.

7

PRAYING WITH LITTLE ONES

Victoria Beech shares some lovely ideas about how to pray with little children (see *www.godventure.co.uk*). One suggestion is to get a scrapbook and glue pictures of people you know on each page. This could include family members, such as grandparents or close friends. Depending on your child's age, you could ask them to flick through the pages to find people they would like to pray for and add a sticker to represent their prayer. Coloured stickers could denote different prayers – for example, red for blessing from God, blue for healing, green for help at work or school, yellow for them to know Jesus is close to them.

8

CREATIVE PRAYER

I am a strong believer in creativity and prayer. I have loved taking my kids to 24/7 prayer rooms for an hour where they have been able to use their imagination to make or paint prayers. Things the girls have done include making a plasticine model of something they wanted to ask God to do in the world and painting a picture of God in heaven.

Getty images

9

NATURE WALKS OR MINI PILGRIMAGES

Looking at the beauty of creation is a wonderful starting point for prayers with our kids. Go for a walk and let them collect bugs, look at the intricacy of a leaf or climb a tree – and then give thanks to God the Creator. And why not visit an old church and encourage the children to think about all the prayers that have been said there over the centuries. You could then join in together as a family with a prayer of your own.

ANDY

Exploring the Bible

The thought of reading the Bible can be daunting for many adults let alone children, but it is through Scripture that God has been revealed to us, so it's important to help our kids read and engage with the Bible. Giving them a love for the Word of God will put them in good stead for their faith journey.

It fascinates me that the Bible is not just a book of rules and regulations; ultimately, it tells a story. Here are some practical ideas to help our children understand the overarching narrative of Scripture and fall in love with the stories of Jesus. Here are a few ideas you might like to try out.

1 CHILDREN AND YOUNG PEOPLE'S BIBLES

With so many brilliant kids' Bibles available now, it might be an idea to give your child a new version specific for their age, hoping that they'll end up with one version they'll grow to love and which will end up well-worn. As you do this, point out one of your favourite stories.

2 LISTENING TO THE BIBLE

Play an audio book of Bible stories in the car or just before bedtime.

3 RE-ENACTING BIBLE STORIES

We can give our children opportunities to engage with the Bible through play. For example, getting all the teddies in the house together and acting out the story of the lost sheep.

4 USING THEIR IMAGINATION

Take time to find an age-appropriate Bible translation for your children so that they can really understand the stories. Introduce the story and then try to bring it to life for them. Get them to picture the scene – the sights, smells and sounds. Take this further by asking them 'I wonder ...' questions such as: 'I wonder what it would have sounded like when Jesus went to Jairus' house and found people wailing because the little girl had died?'

'I wonder ...' statements allow children to explore the emotions of the people in the stories. They can imagine how Zaccheus felt as Jesus looked at him in the tree or how Peter felt as he walked on the water. When reading Old Testament stories, we can also ask the question, 'I wonder how God felt about this?'

5 SINGING SCRIPTURE

Children love songs and a range of excellent kids' worship CDs is available. Often they unpack biblical stories or verses and you can bring these into everyday life – singing to a newborn, listening to some worship in the car, or watching a YouTube clip at home, for example. You might like to use the song as a stepping-stone to reading a psalm or reading the original story that the song is based upon.

6 FAMILY DEVOTIONS

Try out a weekly get-together when you read a story from the Bible and then talk about it. Jo likes to encourage our kids to explore it through role play, painting or crafts. She'll ask them to retell the story and to use their imagination to create something they've learned from it, perhaps a particular emotion they felt.

I like to use props like cushions and blankets to set the scene of a story and get the kids to play different roles as I read it out. Our rhythm of life means that we do not have a set time each week for this, but we look for opportunities to take some time out when we can. Sometimes it lasts five minutes, sometimes an hour.

7 BIBLE-READING AIDS

As your children become better at reading, you might like to discover how they can make Bible reading a habit. Explore with them what a devotional time is and then buy them some age-appropriate Bible notes or a journal to note down their reflections.

8 USING APPS

Smartphone and tablet apps are a great means of allowing our children to engage with the Bible. These include games to play that help them connect with the story, some of which are suitable for children as young as four. We can follow this up by asking them what they have learned.

9 APPLYING THE BIBLE

Of course, the Bible is not just a book to read, so we need to demonstrate how to apply what it teaches us. I remember that when one of my children was having regular nightmares, we would pray for her to sleep peacefully, but we also told her the story of how Jesus promised to give his disciples peace (John 14:27).

10 DIFFICULT BITS!

I remember the day our three-year-old came home having heard the story of Abraham almost sacrificing his son Isaac. Nothing had prepared us for the questions she asked as a result! Difficult questions can arise as we read many things in the Bible, and our children won't be immune to the issues! Every part of the Bible tells us a little bit more about God, but it's important that we give our children the overarching story – in other words, the message that the ultimate revelation of God is in Jesus. One way of unpacking Old Testament stories is to look at the main characters and ask our kids a) the ways in which they were like Jesus and b) the ways in which they were *not* like Jesus. The beauty of this is that we are always pointing our kids to look to Jesus.

ANDY

Spiritual traditions and celebrations

The word *tradition* can carry a lot of baggage, but in talking about *spiritual* traditions we are simply referring to things that we do that add deep meaning to the faith of our family. Earlier in this book, we looked at the importance of family traditions in binding the family together as a unit and giving children an added sense of belonging. Likewise, there are certain traditions or rituals that we can introduce in our families to help our kids connect with and have a deeper sense of the importance of belonging to the family of God. They could be weekly activities or annual events and may be directly or indirectly about faith. Here are a few ideas to consider:

1 CHRISTIAN FESTIVALS

Throughout the church year, there are different festivals – the familiar ones of Christmas and Easter as well as some of the less well-known ones such as Pentecost. These different events can give us an opportunity to create some spiritual family traditions that unpack the meaning behind the celebration. During Advent, Jo 'arranges' for two kindness fairies to visit our house each morning with a challenge written on a slip of paper for each child to do something kind for someone. With Christmas having become so focused upon what we get, this simple tradition has helped our kids understand the importance of giving. Other dates you might like to create a ritual around could be the Passover meal where you talk through the meaning of each item of food, or eating a birthday cake at Pentecost in celebration of the Church's birthday.

Innovation Photography

2 A WEEKLY/MONTHLY FAMILY MEAL

Having a regular meal together and bringing some special elements to it is an opportunity to connect with God as a family. You might like to set aside one night a week or a month to have a favourite meal, maybe lay the table nicely, and take time for each person to share one thing they would like prayer for in the week ahead. Or you could build on the Jewish custom of having a *Shabbat* (Sabbath) meal on Friday nights using candles, water, bread and wine to create a multisensory time of worship together. You can read more about this on the Godventure website (see Resources section).

---

3 RITES OF PASSAGE

A rite of passage is a transition from one phase of life to another – in particular, it marks the changes from childhood to adulthood. Celebrating these occasions are good ways of helping our children to feel a sense of belonging and remember that God will be with them in the next stage of their journey. We might give them a new Bible as they move from primary to secondary school, or we could invite their friends and family to thank God for them, naming their gifts and characteristics, while lighting the candles on their birthday cake.

My friend took his 11-year-old son away to climb a mountain and camp over night. During this one-to-one time, as they walked and lit fires and drank hot chocolate, he talked with his son about six values that were important to him and what they meant in terms of being a man. At the end of the trip, he gave his son a dog tag with the values engraved on it. The weekend was a profound marker in that young man's spiritual journey.

If you decide to create a rites of passage celebration for your child, here are a few top tips:

- Make it an experience. Do something that is special that will be remembered.
- Try to step away from normality – perhaps marking the event in a completely new environment for your child or giving them an experience they've never had before.
- Incorporate some sort of ritual – for example, passing on a family heirloom or reading a special prayer together.
- Involve other adults, to encourage your child with words of wisdom on their faith journey.
- When your child returns after a rites of passage experience, involve friends, family and your church in acknowledging that a shift has taken place. Consider whether you need to change some of the expectations you have of your child, and explore whether they could carry out a new role in church or family life.

'Celebrating these occasions are good ways of helping our children to feel a sense of belonging.'

4 CELEBRATING SPIRITUAL MILESTONES

Just as we celebrate birthdays and anniversaries, we can look out for milestones in our life of faith to enjoy together as a family. For example, we could create some special traditions to mark occasions such as when a child is christened or dedicated, baptised or takes their first communion. Maybe we could even make a note of the date and celebrate the anniversary in years to come if appropriate.

Getty Images

Belonging at church

ANDY

We often talk about going to church, but really that's a bad way of putting it because *we* are the church. When we 'go to church', what we mean is that we are gathering together as followers of Jesus. It's important that our children understand this nuance. As a family, we may go off to different locations during the week, but we do not stop being a family. The church is the community to which we belong.

Helping our children feel that they belong to the church community is important for two reasons: it's about them building relationships and finding their role.

1 GIVING OUR CHILDREN A ROLE IN SUNDAY WORSHIP

There's been a tendency in recent years to choose a local church according to what we can get out of it, but being part of a church community is also about what we can put into it.

There are lots of ways in which we can do this. It might be that our kids can help collect the offering or do one of the readings as they get older. I know that doing a Bible reading each term made me feel that I really belonged in my local church. And if our kids are still young, perhaps we can find a way for them to serve alongside us such as welcoming people into the service or setting up the teas and coffees.

2 INVOLVING THEM IN THE CHURCH ACTIVITIES

When the church is scattered during the week, it can be harder to help our kids still feel that they belong to the church community. With younger children, we may like to do this by attending a church parent and toddler group or, for dads, a Saturday morning group like Who Let the Dads Out, but if not, then it might be worth thinking through how else we can foster this sense of belonging.

As a child, I vividly remember visiting elderly people from the church midweek with my mum. The act of seeing people from church on Sunday morning in their own homes during the week was powerful in cementing relationships. But my mum also took the time to explain to me why we were doing it: it was part of what it was to be the church. As a family, we would also remember people from church in our prayers, again echoing the importance of the community to which we belonged.

Investing in relationships is key, but we can also foster our child's sense of belonging to the church very practically by taking part in its mission. That could involve baking cakes for a community project, helping to collect litter around the edge of the building, or handing out flyers at nursery to a church event.

3 BEWARE OF NEGATIVITY

Perhaps the biggest danger when it comes to damaging children's sense of belonging to the church is the way in which we talk about it. Over the Sunday roast, it's very easy to pick apart the issues we have with the worship or the sermon rather than celebrating what was good. Our negativity can be infectious, and when we are frustrated with certain things at church it's important to think about how we talk about that at home.

ANDY

Parenting in the pew

The challenges of Sunday worship

Sitting in the main service wit children can be a real challe Some churches brilliantly in kids in the prayers and worship bu others expect them to sit quietly. S often as parents, we spend the tim trying to worship while bribing our with snacks and iPhones to keep th quiet. It can be truly frustrating to round and see everyone else lost i worship while our child is beside u exclaiming how bored they are!

Getty Images

There is a challenge here for how churches engage with kids during church services and perhaps it's worth mentioning the reality of this struggle to your church leader. Little things they may not have thought of can make a difference. For instance, Jo and I have been to a church where just the availability of some flags has allowed our kids to integrate more into the worship experience.

However, there will inevitably be times when the worship just goes over our kids' heads, particularly if they are small, and perhaps it's no wonder they get bored. I've been challenged to better explain to my kids what is going on, especially if we are visiting different churches where everything is unfamiliar. I try to give a running commentary on what is happening and why. I take time to explain the pictures in the stained glass windows, the images on the projector screen, the purpose of the written prayers, and why some people raise their hands as they sing. In particular, explaining things like communion and the offering are important in helping them understand what the Christian faith is all about. These simple descriptions have definitely helped my children to understand what is going on and have sparked some good little reflections (although the fact cannot be ignored that a packet of raisins is very effective too!).

HELPING CHILDREN ENGAGE CREATIVELY

Jo is particularly good at packing a concoction of resources into her handbag: crayons, coloured paper, stickers and Pritt stick. Having some backup resources for church has helped to keep our kids quiet, but it has also been a way to help them engage with the service creatively.

'Everyone else is lost in worship while our child is beside us exclaiming how bored they are!'

For example, if we are singing about God's love, we might ask our kids to draw or make something that represents his love, or if we are praying for a broken world, we might ask them to make something as a form of prayer. Rather than asking them to make something specific, like a cross or a picture of Jesus, we can let them creatively respond to a theme. In doing so, they are better able to enter into what is happening.

NB I would be failing in my duty if I didn't give you a word of warning: if you bring an exciting bag of resources, be prepared to find yourself surrounded with other children before too long!

Living out our faith

The Christian faith is very much about connecting with God, but it is also about how we engage with the world. I liken it to breathing in and out: we breathe in, receiving from God, and we breathe out, blessing the world around us.

Living out our faith in the home means that we show Jesus to our children through what we say and do. We shouldn't give them the impression that this is a chore, rather that it is a natural response to God's goodness in our lives. Here are a few ideas about putting this into practice.

ANDY

1 USING GIFTS

God has created each of us as unique individuals with a unique set of gifts, and one of the ways in which we can nurture our children's faith is to help them discover the gifts that God has given them. How they can use these to bless others is a really simple way of demonstrating how we live out our faith. For example, if our child is great at colouring, we could ask them to make a card for a friend who is unwell and talk about how we can use our gifts to help or encourage others.

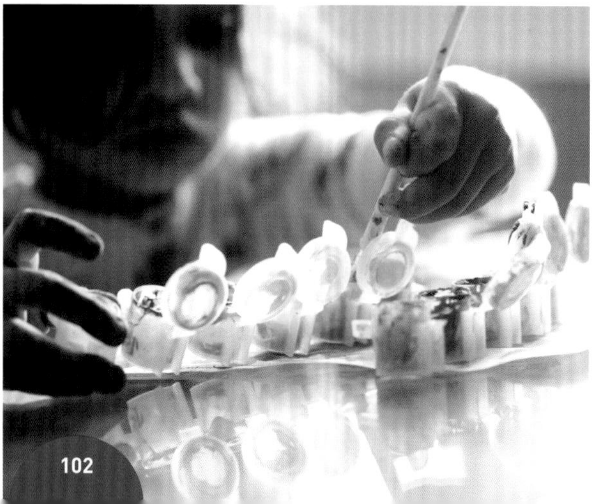
Getty Images

2 LIVING GENEROUSLY

The world is a very broken place, and although we want to protect our kids from the harrowing news stories that come out every day, we do need to begin making them aware of the injustices in the world. Ideas to help our kids learn about the difference they can make to others might include sponsoring an underprivileged child or supporting a school overseas and sending letters and home-made birthday cards. Or, to show the importance of living generously, you could sponsor older children in an activity raising funds for a local cause.

3 SHARING FAITH

As kids begin to interact with other children in nursery and school, we can take the opportunity to help them explore the power of the words they speak. Our kids should never feel pressured, but they might want to share their faith with others. When we are talking to them about how God loves them and values them, we might like to encourage them to tell their friends how important they are to God. Or it might be that they want to invite their friends to church. Giving our children the permission and the language to do this can help equip them. I remember that when my brother was aged six, he suggested to the whole class that they pray for a child who was poorly. A quite bemused teacher agreed!

4 MAKING A STAND

Our faith can be evident in the very ordinary things that we do by habit, and to help our children see that it is practical, it's worth explaining to them *why* we are doing those things. It could be explaining why we are buying Fair Trade products in the supermarket or talking about caring for the earth God has made as we do the recycling.

5 MONEY

At some point, many kids begin to ask about pocket money! A simple thing we have introduced to teach biblical principles about money to my five-year-old is to give her three money tins: one for saving, one for giving and one for spending.

Final thoughts

'One generation commends your work to another; they tell of your mighty acts.'

Psalm 145:4

This is the book that I wished someone had written when our children were little. As parents, Richard and I have learned some lessons the hard way. Looking back, had we known then what we know now, we (and our children!) might have been saved much angst and a good deal of misguided effort and guilt. I'm sure that it would also have given us a freedom to share our faith right in the midst of the busyness and messiness of family life. Most importantly, we would have discovered the incredible truth that at the end of the day it is not all down to us. Paul writes to the Christians in Corinth:

'I planted the seed, Apollos watered it, but God has been making it grow' (1 Corinthians 3:6).

Our hope and prayer is that this book has given lots of encouragement on how to be intentional in planting and watering seeds of faith in our children's lives. It's good to remind ourselves that it is only God who can make those seeds grow ... but we get to partner with him in that incredible task!

THE POWER OF PRAYER

We've shared many parenting principles and practical tips throughout the book, but we've saved the most important lesson until last. The truth is that we can do as much sowing, planting and watering as we like, but ultimately what will really make a difference is engaging in the power of prayer. God's total desire is for his children to be in a relationship with him. So we can know without doubt that when we pray this for our children, we are praying right in the centre of his will for their lives.

From their earliest days, Richard and I have tried to take a moment to pray for our four children every day. We used to pray for them all together in a pack, but we came to discover the power of praying for them as individuals, bringing their specific needs and requests before God.

'Pray in the Spirit on all occasions with all kinds of prayers and requests.'

Ephesians 6:18

As well as immediate issues – health concerns, fallings-out in the playground, struggles at school – as parents we can try to look up and out and pray bigger things for our children's lives. We can look to the promises in the Bible and pray Scripture over them; we can pray ancient prayers of blessing; we can pray for Christian friends and people of influence to come across their paths at just the right time. We can pray for their character and for the fruits of the Spirit – love, joy, peace, patience, kindness, goodness, faithfulness, gentleness and self-control. We can pray they will have wisdom to make good choices and that they will be emotionally strong and able to recover from set-backs. We can pray for their future jobs, relationships and marriage partners – the possibilities are endless. But above all else, we can pray that they have soft hearts that respond to God's love for them.

The Bible tells us to pray 'on all occasions with all kinds of prayers and requests' (Ephesians 6:18). There is no one or right way of praying that suits us all – our different personalities mean that we'll find it easier to pray in different ways. Introverts may love praying on their own in their room with the door closed – what Jesus called 'the secret place'. Those of us with more extrovert tendencies may find that extra challenging – though even we will need some time alone, but we can also pray using everyday family life as a prompt. We can pray for a particular child while tidying their room, or we might tiptoe into their room at night and say a short prayer of blessing over them while they sleep (not recommended for light sleepers!). We can pray as we sort out their clothes from the wash or as we load individual cups or bowls into the dishwasher. When one of my children has been going through a difficult time, I have often put their photo on my phone's home screen. So every time I text, tweet, or take a call their picture is a reminder to pray. Be creative about setting up your own prompts to pray!

WE'RE PLAYING A LONG GAME

It has been wisely said of bringing up children that, 'The days are long, but the years are short.' As any parent of adult children will tell you, the pre-school and primary years do go by so fast, so just as we nurture our children's physical and emotional development, let's try to seize every opportunity we can to sow seeds of faith in our children's lives in their early years.

The truth is that our task as parents is not to raise children or even teenagers, but to raise adults. This is a long game – something that is counter-intuitive in our instant, same-day, uber-society. These seeds of faith that are planted in our children's young lives will slowly bear fruit and produce a harvest in the years to come. We can trust that their Father, the gardener, will play his part, and we can play our part in that process by praying – as people have prayed throughout the ages – that our children would know and respond as we have to his amazing love for them.

'I pray that out of his glorious riches he may strengthen you with power through his Spirit in your inner being, so that Christ may dwell in your hearts through faith. And I pray that you, being rooted and established in love, may have power, together with all the Lord's holy people, to grasp how wide and long and high and deep is the love of Christ, and to know this love that surpasses knowledge – that you may be filled to the measure of all the fullness of God.

Now to him who is able to do immeasurably more than all we ask or imagine, according to his power that is at work within us, to him be glory in the church and in Christ Jesus throughout all generations, for ever and ever! Amen' (Ephesians 3:16–21).

Katharine.

Further resources and support

THE KITCHEN TABLE PROJECT

The Kitchen Table Project from Care for the Family aims to encourage parents as they seek to inspire and nurture their children's faith. We are developing resources and building a growing movement of mums and dads who can join together to share ideas, learn from and support each other.

1. JOIN OUR ONLINE COMMUNITY OF PARENTS

Sign up to be part of the online community and to receive regular encouragement and practical tips for nurturing children's faith. We'll also let you know about any events happening near you and share ideas on how to keep talking and praying with other parents you know.
www.kitchentable.org.uk/join

2. HOST AN INSPIRE SESSION

Our Inspire session is an easy-to-run small group that starts the conversation about nurturing faith in our children. It is designed to be fun, relaxed and interactive, allowing parents to share ideas and experiences.

To host a session:

- Invite a small group of parents to your home or church for a couple of hours.
- Download our leader's guide, video and discussion cards.
- Enjoy talking and learning together.

Everything you need to run a session is free to download at *www.kitchentable.org.uk/inspire.*

SPREAD THE NEWS ABOUT US AT CHURCH

Don't keep it to yourself! Tell other parents and carers at church about the Kitchen Table Project. Go to *www.kitchentable.org.uk/church* to find posters, leaflets, and a church toolkit that includes sermon outlines, discussion questions and ways to equip parents to share their faith at home.

FOLLOW US ON SOCIAL MEDIA

Chat to other parents, share ideas and experiences, find out about everything that's going on and keep up to date with all our new resources.

/ktpcampaign   @ktpcampaign

CARE FOR THE FAMILY

Care for the Family is a national charity which aims to strengthen family life and help those who face family difficulties. We provide parenting, relationship and bereavement support through events, courses, training, a volunteer network and other resources.

Visit *www.careforthefamily.org.uk* to find out more about our resources, support and training. This covers a range of areas including:

- Couple relationships
- Parenting
- Families with additional needs children
- Bereaved parents and siblings
- Single parents
- Young widows/widowers
- Parent and toddler group leaders
- Marriage preparation

/careforthefamily @care4thefamily

OTHER RESOURCES

Visit *www.kitchentable.org.uk/resources* for ideas and links to useful resources. Here are a few to get you started.

WEBSITES

Parenting for Faith – *www.parentingforfaith.org*
Videos, articles and resources to equip parents to help children and teenagers develop a lasting and vibrant two-way relationship with God. The Parenting for Faith course can be downloaded free of charge.

Godventure – *www.godventure.org.uk*
Creative ideas and resources for prayer activities, Bible activities, and exploring God through play.

Guardians of Ancora – *www.guardiansofancora.com*
A free game-app from Scripture Union for children aged 8 to 11 to help them explore Bible stories and their relationship with God.

BOOKS

Parenting Children for a Life of Faith
Rachel Turner, BRF
Clear and practical suggestions to help children develop a personal faith, not just knowledge about faith. The book explores how to proactively disciple our children, model the reality of being in a relationship with God, and connect children to God's heart. Full of encouragement and real-life help.

Sticky Faith: Everyday Ideas to Build Lasting Faith in Your Kids
Kara E. Powell and Chap Clark, Zondervan
An encouraging and useful guide for parents about helping children move from childhood faith to a faith that is uniquely theirs. Includes practical ideas and questions to help apply the material at home.